S. Hrg. 113–629

SYRIA AFTER GENEVA: NEXT STEPS FOR U.S. POLICY

HEARING

BEFORE THE

COMMITTEE ON FOREIGN RELATIONS UNITED STATES SENATE

ONE HUNDRED THIRTEENTH CONGRESS

SECOND SESSION

MARCH 26, 2014

Printed for the use of the Committee on Foreign Relations

Available via the World Wide Web: http://www.gpo.gov/fdsys/

U.S. GOVERNMENT PUBLISHING OFFICE

94–280 PDF   WASHINGTON : 2015

(II)

CONTENTS

SYRIA AFTER GENEVA: NEXT STEPS FOR U.S. POLICY

WEDNESDAY, MARCH 26, 2014

U.S. SENATE,
COMMITTEE ON FOREIGN RELATIONS,
Washington, DC.

The committee met, pursuant to notice, at 2:40 p.m., in room SD–419, Dirksen Senate Office Building, Hon. Robert Menendez (chairman of the committee) presiding.

Present: Senators Menendez, Coons, Murphy, Kaine, Corker, and McCain.

OPENING STATEMENT OF HON. ROBERT MENENDEZ, U.S. SENATOR FROM NEW JERSEY

The CHAIRMAN. Good afternoon.

We are here today with a distinguished panel of experts to hear their views and express our concerns about what Congress can do about Syria after Geneva.

At the moment, there is clearly a stalemate at the political level. The Geneva II process failed to achieve any forward momentum and fell far short of the goal to agree on a transitional governing body. The Syrian opposition delegation went to Geneva ready to work responsibly on behalf of the Syrian people and Assad's delegation demonstrated their contempt for international efforts to medi ate an end to the violence and preserve what is left of Syria.

If there was any doubt about the true character of this regime, it was brought into sharp focus when Assad went after family members of the opposition following Geneva. Meanwhile, the barrel bombs continue to drop. The starvation and torture campaign went on unabated, even while the delegations were sitting at the negotiating table.

Assad has shown that he is willing to fight to the last Syrian.

Meanwhile, the international community seems paralyzed on what to do next. This hearing is about exactly that. What is next in Syria? And I hope to explore with our panelists new thinking, new options, to hear some creative new ideas that answer what is next and that can help determine what additional role Congress can play.

The record for this committee for empowering the moderate Syrian opposition and ensuring that a credible military threat is on the table has been clear for some time.

The question before us last week was how to break the stalemate on the ground. With recent regime advances, the question may now be how to reverse their momentum and shore up opposition forces.

Our partners in the Syrian Military Council are now fighting a two-front war, one against al-Qaeda affiliates and extremists who would impose Sharia law, the other against Assad and his security forces that remain loyal to him, Lebanese Hezbollah and Iraqi Shia militias trained in Iran with Iranian equipment and funding, military equipment, and international protection supplied by Russia and direct guidance training and fighters provided by Iran.

In conclusion, I would note that on Monday, U.N. Security Council General Ban Ki Moon reported to the U.N. Security Council on Resolution 2139 that named areas in Syria where the siege must be lifted. Predictably Assad did not meet the demands of the unanimous U.N. Security Council resolution. Hospitals, schools, and other civilian areas are still militarized. Areas are blocked from humanitarian aid and the barrel bombs are still falling.

We need to insist on accountability and make it clear that there are consequences for ignoring the U.N. Security Council. Ultimately, the longer the war continues the fewer options we will have to end the horrific level of violence and the humanitarian nightmare. The loss of an entire generation of Syrian children, the collapse of a society that has given tremendous gifts to the world—this is not a legacy that anyone wants to live with.

Clearly the stakes are high and growing higher every day. We need concerted, decisive U.S. leadership. The fact is we needed it 2 years ago. We needed it yesterday and we need it today.

Before I recognize Senator Corker, I received a letter that both he and I received from the Syrian Opposition Coalition President Ahmad Jarba. Mr. Jarba's message is timely and meaningful. And without objection, I will add it to the record.

[The letter referred to can be found on page 75.]

The CHAIRMAN. In particular, I know Mr. Jarba's commitment to partnering with us on a long-term strategic plan for supporting the moderate opposition and the Syrian Opposition Council's enduring commitment to a political solution, countering terrorism, and the U.N. Security Council resolutions 2118 and 2139.

So we support the struggle for a post-Assad Syria that represents all Syrians.

Also, I believe that there are some individuals who are here from the Syrian Opposition in attendance at today's hearing: Dr. Najib Ghadbian, the Special Representative to the United States for the National Coalition of Syrian Revolution and Opposition Forces; Ms. Rima Fleihan, a member of the opposition's delegation negotiating team in Geneva; Mr. Qusai Zakarya, a survivor of Assad's August 2013 chemical weapons attack and an influential youth activist working every day to make sure the world does not lose sight of the suffering of the Syrian people. We welcome you to the hearing.

And now I would like to recognize the distinguished ranking member for his remarks. Senator Corker.

OPENING STATEMENT OF HON. BOB CORKER,
U.S. SENATOR FROM TENNESSEE

Senator CORKER. Thank you, Mr. Chairman, for having this hearing, and I want to thank the witnesses for their service to our country and apologize for the five votes that we are going to have during this hearing.

This is our fourth hearing on Syria since the committee voted 15–3 to jump-start a comprehensive Syria strategy last May, including authorizing meaningful support to the moderate opposition and imposing sanctions on those who support Assad. Each of these hearings has had a clear, consistent theme. U.S. policy has completely failed to shift the balance of power, improve the humanitarian situation, or achieve the President's stated goal of removing Assad. In fact, I would argue that United States policy in Syria has achieved the exact opposite by making promises of support that were never fulfilled, and that has occurred and we know that. We have allowed Assad to solidify his position, embolden his external supporters, and undermine the moderate opposition.

And in our last hearing on Syria, we heard that this is a civil war. Now this civil war threatens regional stability and has allowed terrorists to control more strategic territory in the heart of the Arab world than they did prior to 9/11.

Faced with this failure, the administration is now required by law to conduct a comprehensive interagency strategy in order to use the funding authorities laid out in the appropriations bill that passed in January. I look forward to seeing the results of this review, but I am not confident it will convince the President who appears to fear provoking Russia and Iran and is not committed to changing the course of the conflict in any real way. And I hope the testimony today will shed light on the Russian-Iranian situation. We will, instead, continue along the current course in Syria, which leads us to a disaster, to quote the Director of National Intelligence.

So while it is important for this committee to highlight the failure in this administration's Syria policy, today I hope we can move beyond this. Today I hope we can use this hearing to generate new policy ideas on Syria, creative alternative legislative proposals for Congress to propose that will move United States policy and, by extension, the future of Syria in a better direction.

And again I thank you for your testimony.

The CHAIRMAN. Thank you, Senator Corker.

Our first panel. We are pleased to welcome Assistant Secretary of State for Near Eastern Affairs Anne Patterson who knows the region extremely well from her long service, and Assistant Secretary of State for International Security and Nonproliferation Tom Countryman.

Let me remind you that both of your statements will be fully included in the record, without objection.

I would ask you to summarize your statements in about 5 minutes or so, so we can have a full discussion. For the purposes of your knowledge, we have four more votes that are pending. So my hope is to get your testimony in and then recess until the end of those four votes so we can have a continuum of discussion.

With that, Madam Secretary, we will recognize you first.

STATEMENT OF HON. ANNE PATTERSON, ASSISTANT SECRETARY OF STATE FOR NEAR EASTERN AFFAIRS, U.S. DEPARTMENT OF STATE, WASHINGTON, DC

Ambassador PATTERSON. Thank you, Mr. Chairman, Ranking Member Corker, for inviting me here today with Tom Countryman.

I am aware that members of this committee are not satisfied with our progress to date. Neither are we. The administration appreciates the concern and support of this committee, most recently expressed in your March 14 letter.

Today I will supplement testimony provided by Deputy Secretary Burns on March 6, and I have provided a full statement for the record.

The popular demands for reform sweeping the Middle East began 3 years ago in Syria's peaceful protests. The Assad regime's response to these demands has torn the nation apart. More than 146,000 people have been killed since the unrest and violence began; 2.5 million people have sought refuge in neighboring countries. Inside Syria, 6.5 million are displaced, and over 9 million in need of humanitarian assistance.

The situation on the ground is constantly in flux. Regime troops get critical battle support from Hezbollah and the Iranian Revolutionary Guard. They have Iranian and Russian weapons, and they resort to barrel bombs or starvation to terrorize civilians.

But peace will not come to Syria from a military victory, only from a negotiated political settlement.

The conflict has attracted experienced foreign fighters who are drawn to the ungoverned regions left by the deterioration of the Assad regime. ODNI staff estimates there are 23,000 violent extremist fighters in Syria, including more than 7,000 foreign fighters. The al-Qaeda-linked Nusra Front and the Islamic State of Iraq and the Levant are the largest groups. They offer weapons and money to Syrian men who oppose the regime but who might not otherwise be drawn to their ranks.

Mr. Chairman, we are reviewing our policy and identifying priorities for coordinated action, and I would like to share some of those with you today.

In Pakistan, we saw the dangers of ungoverned areas that become terrorist safe havens and how difficult it is to end them. A top priority is preventing the establishment of a permanent terrorist safe haven in Syria. In coordination with allies and partners, we are organizing to address the extremist fighters in Syria and we are working to cut their sources of funding and recruits.

We are also working to strengthen the moderate Syrian opposition both inside and outside of Syria because they face a two-front war against both the Assad regime and the violent extremists.

Mr. Chairman, members of this committee have been rightly concerned about the pace and effectiveness of support for the civilian opposition. This has been a challenge since we do not have a direct U.S. Government presence inside the country, as well as control of many border posts by al-Qaeda-linked groups or their offshoots. Our strategy has been to use $260 million in nonlethal assistance to link the Syrian Coalition to councils and NGOs inside the country, helping to unify and strengthen the opposition. Over half of that assistance has been delivered.

Based on our experience over the past year, we have now begun refocusing by directly channeling resources to local governments and civil society groups, as well as the SOC, and to trusted commanders, as well the Supreme Military Council. We are focusing on helping communities maintain basic public services. This strategy allows localities to sustain local institutions that will also be critical to building a post-Assad Syria.

In towns and cities under opposition control, we are beginning to provide cash grants to pay police and teachers. We continue to train local councils and civil society organizations in administration and we are providing heavy equipment.

As part of the $260 million in overall nonlethal assistance, we are providing $80 million in support to the SMC on a very fluid battlefield. Nonlethal assistance requirements are identified by commanders and include food rations, medical kits, as well as communications and other personal gear.

In December, an SMC warehouse in Syria containing United States supplies was overrun by a faction of extremist fighters. We suspended assistance until they reestablished secure supply routes and storage facilities. By February, when the SMC regained control of its facility, we resumed supplies, this time directly to commanders. We will do more in coming months to support the Syrian civilian and armed opposition and civil society groups.

We are supporting Syria's neighbors to contain the conflict. We are providing humanitarian assistance and other support to Lebanon to address border and internal security issues. We are working with Turkey and Jordan on border security, counterterrorism, and humanitarian concerns. We are surging security assistance to help Iraq combat ISIL incursions, and we are coordinating with Israel to monitor threats and support Israel's right to defend itself from spillover violence.

The international community is also working to alleviate the suffering caused by this crisis. The Government of Kuwait and the United Nations cohosted the most recent donor conference in January which resulted in $2.5 billion in new pledges. The United States is the largest single donor, providing more than $1.7 billion in humanitarian assistance. Our challenge is the Assad regime's policy of deliberately blocking humanitarian access to people in need.

Transitioning to a representative government is the only way to reduce the violence and alleviate the suffering of the Syrian people. The international community, including Russia, maintains that the conflict must end via a negotiated political agreement in line with the 2012 Geneva Communique, but the Assad regime has squandered every opportunity.

The United States and Russia share a common interest in a successful negotiation that prevents the spread of instability and violent extremism beyond Syria's borders. However, Russia has done nothing to pressure the Assad regime to advance the Geneva II negotiations, and they are increasing the quantity and the quality of weapons provided to the Syrian regime. We continue to review options for changing President Putin's calculus.

Separately, I know that the safety of Syria's minority communities, including Christians, is a concern for the committee as it is for us. We have sought and received assurances from the Syrian opposition and moderate rebels that they will protect women and minorities and engage them in building Syria's future.

Mr. Chairman, even as we pursue all the steps I have outlined today, we continue to examine what more we can do to defend U.S. interests in Syria and to achieve a political settlement, and we look forward to working with the committee in this respect.

Thank you.

[The prepared statement of Ambassador Patterson follows:]

PREPARED STATEMENT OF AMBASSADOR ANNE W. PATTERSON

Thank you, Mr. Chairman, Ranking Member Corker, and members of the committee, for inviting me today to discuss the crisis in Syria. I am well aware that many members of this committee are not satisfied with our progress to date. Neither are we. Let me say that the administration appreciates your concern and the support this committee has shown for efforts to address this challenge.

The committee heard from Deputy Secretary Burns 3 weeks ago on the challenge of sectarian and extremist violence related to the conflict. Today I will supplement Deputy Secretary Burns' remarks by describing the coordinated strategy that we are developing. I am pleased to be accompanied today by my colleague, Assistant Secretary for International Security and Nonproliferation Tom Countryman, who will address the international community's progress in the removal and destruction of Syria's chemical weapons.

THE CRISIS

The popular demands for economic and political reform sweeping the Middle East began 3 years ago in Syria as peaceful protests. Syria's large youthful population sought an end to oppression and new opportunities. The Assad regime's response to these demands has torn the nation apart, fueling extremism and inflaming regional tensions.

More than 146,000 people have been killed since the unrest and violence began. The number of conflict-affected civilians seeking refuge in neighboring countries has increased to more than 2.5 million people while, inside Syria, an additional 6.5 million people are displaced and at least 9.3 million people are in need of humanitarian assistance. The U.N. Security Council has condemned the denial of humanitarian access to civilians in need and has urged immediate steps to facilitate relief operations throughout the country, yet the regime has continued to obstruct humanitarian access. Again last week, the U.N. Commission of Inquiry on Syria reported on the continuing human rights violations being committed by the regime, as well as human rights abuses by the al-Qaeda linked groups and their offshoots that have taken root in the ungoverned spaces that Assad's actions and atrocities have created.

Opposition to the Assad regime in Syria is broad and deep. Most Syrians who side with the opposition are moderates. In large areas of the country they have thrown off regime control, yet the situation on the ground is constantly in flux. In some areas, regime forces—with Hezbollah and Iranian Revolutionary Guard support—have regained control of territory they had lost earlier in the conflict. Syrian troops are well armed with Iranian and Russian weapons, and also resort to barrel bombs or starvation to terrorize civilians. But peace will not come to Syria from a military victory. The only sustainable solution to the Syria crisis is a negotiated political settlement.

The United States is a leader of the "London 11" contact group that has worked to move forward the Syrian transition, end the violence, and achieve a political solution. Although the U.N.-sponsored Geneva II negotiations have stalled due to regime intransigence aided by the tacit support of Russia, the process served to unify components of the Syrian opposition and to enable it to articulate its vision for a transitional government.

The continuing civil war has proved a magnet for foreign violent extremists—some with substantial combat experience—who are drawn to the ungoverned regions left by the deterioration of the Assad regime. Our colleagues at the Office of the Director of National Intelligence have estimated that there are nearly 23,000 violent extremist fighters in Syria, including more than 7,000 foreign fighters. They represent a minority of the total rebel ranks inside Syria, which are estimated to be between 75,000–110,000 fighters. The violent extremist fighters belong to several groups but most notably al-Qaeda's official affiliate in Syria, Nusra Front, and the

Islamic State of Iraq and the Levant (ISIL), formerly known as al-Qaeda in Iraq, whose new name indicates its growing ambitions. ISIL is responsible for most of the violence that has been taking place in Iraq's Anbar province aimed at destabilizing Iraq. These groups offer weapons and money to Syrian men who oppose the regime, yet who might not otherwise be drawn to violent extremist causes but for the money and avenue for action against the regime they provide.

Bashar al-Assad bears responsibility for this metastasizing problem. His regime has released terrorists from its jails, allowed violent extremist bases to emerge, and invited other foreign terrorist organizations including Lebanese Hezbollah, as well as Iranian-trained militia fighters from Iraq and Pakistan, to join the fight on its side.

Mr. Chairman, we are reviewing our policy and identifying priorities for coordinated action.

COUNTERING VIOLENT EXTREMIST ACTIVITY

In Pakistan, we clearly saw the dangers that arise when terrorists are able to set up safe havens—and how difficult and costly in lives and money it becomes to dislodge or destroy them. For that reason, a top priority in the Syria crisis is preventing the establishment of a permanent terrorist safe-haven. In coordination with allies and partners, we are now better organizing ourselves to address the growing challenge of violent extremist fighters in Syria and the flow of these fighters into and out of the country. With our partners, we will apply tools, tactics, and best practices to mitigate potential threats and build upon existing lines of cooperation.

We are working with members of the opposition, Syria's neighbors and other regional states to cut off their sources of funding and recruits. Saudi Arabia has criminalized participation in foreign conflicts by its citizens and is prosecuting individuals who have done so. Our allies in the gulf increasingly, and correctly, see the flood of violent extremists from their countries as a threat to themselves. We have new initiatives to work with our allies to identify violent extremists who have traveled to the region.

We are also working to strengthen the moderate Syrian opposition, both inside and outside of Syria, because they are now facing a two-front war against both the Assad regime and the violent extremists.

PREVENTING COLLAPSE AND NONLETHAL SUPPORT

In parts of Syria where the regime has been ousted, we want to prevent the wholesale collapse of Syria's institutions and public services and keep regime hardliners and violent extremists from asserting control. As the fighting has continued, the regime has increasingly targeted civilian populations by denying basic services and cutting them off from food, fuel, and medical care. But some provincial and local councils and civil society organizations continue struggling, against great odds, to maintain local government and continue critical services. We need to help them.

Mr. Chairman, members of this committee have been rightly concerned about the pace and effectiveness of support for the civilian opposition. Without a direct U.S. Government presence inside the country—as well as control of many border entry points by al-Qaeda-linked groups or their offshoots—it has been difficult to increase our assistance to the Syrian opposition. Our strategy had been to use $260 million in nonlethal assistance to link the Syrian Coalition (SOC) to councils and NGOs inside the country, helping to unify and strengthen the opposition.

However, based on our experience on the ground over the past year, we have been refocusing our activity. Over the past few months the State Department and USAID have stepped up efforts to channel resources directly to local and provincial governments and civil society groups, as well as the SOC.

Our focus is increasingly on ways to help communities maintain basic security, keep the lights on, provide water, food and basic medical care—staving off the advances of extremist groups who seek to exploit peoples' desperation. It allows these localities to maintain the basic public institutions that will be so critical in rebuilding a post-Assad Syria.

In towns and cities under opposition control, we are beginning to provide cash grants to pay local law enforcement and teachers. We continue to train local councils and civil society organizations in administration and local governance. And we are providing equipment and supplies to help them, including heavy equipment such as generators, cranes, trucks, and ambulances. In one major city, for example, we have helped reopen 17 schools serving 9,300 students. In another major city, we funded the refurbishment of 60 police stations and are providing nonlethal equipment and basic stipends to 1,300 policemen, who are struggling to maintain order.

Paying stipends not only helps keep these people on the job, but it also helps deprive the extremist groups of the chance to fill the vacuum themselves.

Make no mistake: this is extremely difficult work and nobody is saying that this assistance will turn the tide against what remains an extremely serious and deteriorating situation. As we learned in Iraq—even with 160,000 American troops, 10 years of effort, tens of thousands of schools refurbished, and hundreds of millions of dollars spent-it takes generations to restore stability in societies wrecked by decades of dictatorship and civil wars. We are determined, however, to stand with those struggling to rebuild and stabilize their local communities even in the most horrific circumstances imaginable. These brave individuals will be the future leaders of Syria; they deserve our support, and they will continue to receive it through the types of assistance I just described.

As part of this $260 million in nonlethal overall assistance, moreover, we are providing $80 million in support to the Supreme Military Command (SMC). Providing this support to groups engaged in a highly fluid battle zone has been challenging. In December, an SMC warehouse in Syria containing U.S. supplies was overrun by a faction of extremist fighters. We suspended SMC assistance until they could reestablish secure supply routes and storage facilities. By February, when the SMC regained control of its facility and accounted for its contents, we began sending supplies again—this time directly to trusted commanders.

In providing nonlethal assistance to the SMC, needs are identified by commanders and have included food rations, medical kits, and vehicles—as well as communications and other personal gear. These supplies not only fill gaps identified by opposition troops fighting both the regime and violent extremists, but they are tangible evidence of our support for the moderate opposition.

Although a leadership debate has opened up within the SMC—as the Syrian opposition discusses how to fight the regime more effectively—the dispute has not affected our ability to deliver nonlethal assistance to the moderate armed opposition through trusted commanders.

None of the nonlethal assistance we are providing will be determinative in defeating regime forces, nor will it, on its own, force Assad to change his calculus about trying to hold on to power. However, our assistance does provide needed equipment while sending a signal both to those inside and outside Syria of our strong support for the moderate opposition; help maintain basic administrative institutions; help prevent the formation of vacuums in services and security that extremists aggressively exploit; and create relationships with moderates who can, when this conflict is over, form the basis of a transitional government.

ELIMINATING THE THREAT OF CHEMICAL WEAPONS

The Assad regime used chemical weapons against its citizens, and its continued possession of chemical weapons material represents a sustained danger to Syria's population and all of its neighbors, including Israel. Last year, the international community, led by the United States and Russia, united to defend a longstanding international norm against the use of chemical weapons. Under a Joint Mission organized by the United Nations and the Organization for the Prohibition of Chemical Weapons (OPCW), the international community is supporting the safe elimination of Syria's chemical weapons program. U.S. assistance includes outfitting a vessel to neutralize Syria's highest priority chemical precursors and agents.

We are making progress, but there is tough work ahead. To date, the Joint Mission has verified the destruction of Syria's chemical weapons-production equipment, the machines that mix the components, and the removal of nearly half of Syria's declared stockpile. All of the sulfur mustard agent and some of the precursors for sarin, the highest priority declared chemicals, have now been removed. It is our goal to complete the removal of declared chemicals as soon as possible in April and the verified destruction of these chemical weapons and materials by June 30.

PROTECTING OUR FRIENDS AND ALLIES

We are committed to helping contain the conflict by bolstering the security and stability of Syria's neighbors. Violence from the ongoing conflict has already spilled into Lebanon and Turkey, our NATO ally. Recently, Israel retaliated against Syrian Army targets for an attack on an Israeli patrol on the Golan Heights. On Sunday, the Turkish Air Force shot down a Syrian plane that had encroached along the border. ISIL has used its position in Syria to pour extremist fighters and weapons into Iraq. Lebanon and Jordan are bearing an enormous burden as they work to secure their borders and meet the needs of more than 1.6 million refugees from Syria. We appreciate the support we have received from Congress as we work directly and with our international partners to support Syria's neighbors:

- We back the Lebanese Government's efforts to contain the Syrian conflict and strongly condemn Hezbollah's intervention on behalf of the Assad regime. The U.S. has provided additional support to the Lebanese Armed Forces and Internal Security Forces to help them secure Lebanon's borders and address internal security threats. We are helping the Lebanese Government care for nearly 1 million refugees from Syria and strengthen the communities that are hosting them. We have provided more than $340 million in humanitarian assistance to support the needs of these refugees and to reduce the burden on Lebanese communities. In addition, our ongoing bilateral assistance is helping to address deteriorating economic conditions and gaps in the delivery of important services, particularly in communities impacted by the crisis.

  - Many of you met with Jordan's King Abdullah when he was here recently and can appreciate the contributions that Jordan is making to address this crisis. The United States is already working closely with the Jordanian Armed Forces (JAF) to address threats emanating from Syria, including providing enhanced border security and counterterrorism capabilities. DOD funds also help to assist the JAF with providing humanitarian assistance to newly arriving Syrian refugees. Longstanding development programs help relieve the strains on water infrastructure, schools, and health facilities in Jordanian communities that support large numbers of Syrian refugees. We have provided $300 million in additional budget support over the last 2 years and will support a $1 billion loan guarantee for Jordan as well as the renewal of our bilateral assistance Memorandum of Understanding for an additional 5 years, as announced by the President last month.
- In regards to Turkey, we are most importantly working with Ankara on a variety of counterterrorism issues to address the growing threat that Syria-based terrorists pose to Turkey and the challenge posed by foreign fighters. Additionally, Turkey hosts far more than the 641,000 officially registered refugees from Syria, in addition to significant parts of the Syrian opposition leadership. We are working to mitigate the Syrian conflict's spillover on Turkey's security and sovereignty, including through the deployment of two U.S. Patriot batteries in southern Turkey, which join four batteries from other NATO allies. U.S. contributions to the international humanitarian response help provide critical support to refugees hosted in Turkish camps and communities. In support of the U.N., Turkey is playing an important role in facilitating cross-border humanitarian assistance in northern Syria.
- Iraq hosts more than 225,000 refugees from Syria, mostly in the Iraqi Kurdistan region. Since 2012, the United States has provided more than $90 million in humanitarian aid to international organizations and NGOs for Syrian refugees in Iraq. We are also working with the U.N. and the Iraqi Government to ensure that the estimated 350,000 Iraqis displaced by the Anbar conflict are getting needed assistance and will be able to vote in Iraq's upcoming elections, which ISIL seeks to disrupt. At the same time, we are in close contact with Iraq's political leaders and security commanders to develop and execute a holistic campaign to isolate ISIL from the population, including through intensified information sharing and security assistance.
- In Egypt, which hosts over 135,000 Syrian refugees, political instability and polarization has contributed to a difficult environment and increasing humanitarian needs for refugees. Recognizing the burden that refugee communities can pose on host countries, we are continuing to support humanitarian partners in Egypt and to engage the government to ensure that refugees receive needed support.
- Israel has not been spared the effects of the conflict. Our governments coordinate closely to monitor violent extremist threats in Syria, and we support Israel's right to defend itself from spillover violence. We applaud Israeli efforts to provide medical care to wounded Syrians seeking help. We are also concerned that Syria's instability will continue to threaten the Golan.

URGENT HUMANITARIAN ACTION

We are coordinating closely with the international community to alleviate the suffering caused by this crisis. The Government of Kuwait cohosted a donor conference with the U.N. Secretary General in January, which resulted in $2.6 billion in new pledges. The United States is the largest single donor to the Syria humanitarian response, providing more than $1.7 billion in humanitarian assistance. Our assistance supports U.N. and other international organizations as well as numerous NGOs assisting conflict-affected civilians inside the country and throughout the region. We are specifically directing some of our funds to alleviate the growing strain on host communities, infrastructure and public services in neighboring countries. Inside Syria, our assistance provides food, basic health care, water and sanitation services, and desperately needed relief supplies.

The Assad regime continues to deliberately block humanitarian access in Syria, citing the uncertain security situation. Last week, the first U.N. convoy reached the residents of Qamishli in northern Syria via the Turkish border crossing at Nusaybin. Although some supplies will finally reach these people in desperate need, one day of U.N. aid convoys crossing one border point is not enough. These convoys prove that the Syrian Army can allow humanitarian access when it chooses to do so. The Assad regime must approve all U.N. requests for access to areas in need immediately as called for by the U.N. Security Council.

NEGOTIATIONS TRANSITIONING TO A REPRESENTATIVE GOVERNMENT

Transitioning to a representative government that is responsive to the needs of the Syrian people is the only way to reduce the violence and alleviate the suffering of the Syrian people. While the international community, including Russia, maintains that the conflict must end via a negotiated political agreement in line with the 2012 Geneva Communique, the regime has squandered every opportunity for a peaceful settlement. At the Geneva II talks, the regime's negotiator insulted the opposition, U.N. Joint Special Representative Lakhdar Brahimi and the international community while contributing nothing of substance to the discussion.

The United States and Russia share a common interest in a successful negotiation that fully implements the Geneva Communique and prevents the spread of instability and violent extremism beyond Syria's borders. To date, this common interest has motivated Russia to continue its support to the OPCW mission. However, Russia has done nothing to move its Syrian allies forward in the Geneva II negotiations. Moreover, we have seen an increase in both the quantity and the quality of weapons Russia has provided to the Syrian regime in recent months. The stability that Russia seeks in Syria will not be achieved by providing planes, tanks, bombs, and guns for use against the Syrian people. We continue to review all options for changing President Putin's calculus away from Russia's support for the Assad regime.

Ambassador Brahimi told the Security Council on March 13, that he recommends against a third round of talks unless the regime commits to discuss substantively all elements of the Geneva Communique. In the meantime, the United States and its partners will continue to expand our support to the Syrian opposition and ratchet up pressure on the regime.

On another matter, I know that the safety of Syria's minority communities is a key concern for members of this committee, as it is for us. We are troubled by the plight of all civilians in Syria, including Christians and other religious minorities. Protecting the security and religious rights of these communities, as well as the rights of women, is an important element of our policy and will be essential to any future political settlement. We have sought and received assurances from the Syrian opposition leadership and moderate rebel leaders that they will protect the rights of women and minorities, and engage them in plans for building Syria's future.

NEXT STEPS

Mr. Chairman, we are actively engaged in trying to bring the Syria crisis to an end.
—We are working with allies and partners to combat the growing threat of violent extremists;
—We are working to prevent a catastrophic collapse of Syrian cities in opposition controlled areas;
—We are providing nonlethal support to the armed opposition;
—We are working with the international community to end the threat of Syria's chemical weapons;
—We are taking steps to protect and support our regional friends and allies;
—We are contributing generously to the humanitarian response both inside Syria and among its neighbors; and
—We are providing support to the Syrian opposition both directly and through the London 11.

Even as we pursue all the steps I have outlined today, we continue to examine what more we can do to defend U.S. interests in Syria and to achieve a political settlement. We appreciate the support of your committee—most recently in your March 14 letter—and will continue to work together with the Congress as we move forward.

The Syrian people reject violent extremism. They want to return home and rebuild their country—and we will help them. Thank you.

The CHAIRMAN. Thank you.

Secretary Countryman.

STATEMENT OF HON. THOMAS M. COUNTRYMAN, ASSISTANT SECRETARY FOR INTERNATIONAL SECURITY AND NON-PROLIFERATION, U.S. DEPARTMENT OF STATE, WASHINGTON, DC

Mr. COUNTRYMAN. I thank the chairman and the ranking member for the opportunity to appear with Assistant Secretary Patterson and to testify on one specific aspect of the Syrian situation, that is, the complete elimination of Syria's chemical weapons. I will be brief.

Since Secretary Kerry negotiated the framework last September to eliminate these weapons, we have made important progress, but much remains to be done. Thanks to an impressive international coalition, almost half of Syria's declared chemical weapons materials are out of Syria, including the entire declared stockpile of sulfur mustard. International inspectors have conducted full inspections of the declared chemical weapons sites and have verified the destruction of Syria's chemical weapons production, mixing, and filling equipment.

This recent momentum is significant but the most significant moment will be when all of these terrible weapons are out of the hands of the regime so they cannot be used again against the Syrian people.

The task before us remains considerable. Sixty-five percent of the most dangerous chemicals—Priority 1 chemicals—have yet to be removed from Syria. We continue to work with the international community to maintain pressure on the regime to move faster. We have made clear that the agreed schedules are not up for renegotiation and that the elimination effort must be completed as quickly and safely as possible.

The regime missed the March 15th date for the physical destruction of production facilities. We intend to hold them to this and other international obligations. If Syria meets the agreed schedule for removal, the overall June 30th target date for the complete elimination of the program remains achievable. The next few weeks are critical and we and the rest of the world will be watching. There are simply no logistical or security reasons that the Assad regime cannot complete the removal effort next month.

As the removal and elimination process continues, we will redouble our support for the OPCW's verification and inspection efforts to ensure the accuracy and completeness of Syria's declarations. The United States approaches this process with our eyes wide open. Following removal of declared chemicals, further review and verification of Syria's declaration of its program will be required in order to achieve international confidence that the program has been completely eliminated.

I thank you and I look forward to any questions you may have.

[The prepared statement of Mr. Countryman follows:]

PREPARED STATEMENT OF ASSISTANT SECRETARY THOMAS M. COUNTRYMAN

Chairman Menendez, Ranking Member Corker, and members of the committee, thank you for the opportunity to testify today about international efforts to support the United Nations (U.N.) and the Organisation for the Prohibition of Chemical

Weapons (OPCW) in the complete and verifiable elimination of the Syrian chemical weapons program. While we have made important progress in the past months toward the elimination of Syria's chemicals weapons program, considerable work remains to be done to ensure the Assad regime can never again use these terrible weapons against its own people, or threaten our regional and international partners with them.

Just last year, the regime did not even publicly acknowledge that it possessed chemical weapons, despite having used them on multiple occasions, including in attacks that killed over 1,400 people. Today, OPCW inspectors on the ground in Syria, with U.N. support, have conducted full inspections of Syria's declared chemical weapons-related sites, and have verified the functional destruction of the chemical weapons production, mixing, and filling equipment at those sites. In addition, as of today, more than 49 percent of Syria's declared chemical weapons materials slated for destruction outside of Syria have been removed, including all of Syria's declared sulfur mustard agent, and the OPCW has verified the destruction in Syria of 93 percent of Syria's declared isopropanol, a binary component of the nerve agent sarin. But that's not good enough. Syria has yet to remove 65 percent of its most dangerous (Priority 1) declared chemicals. We must continue to work with the international community to maintain pressure on the Assad regime to remove all of these chemicals as urgently as possible.

The international community has established a firm legal framework, through U.N. Security Council Resolution (UNSCR) 2118 and decisions of the OPCW Executive Council, to ensure that this immense undertaking is completed in a transparent, expeditious, and verifiable manner, with a target for destroying all of Syria's declared chemicals by June 30 of this year.

The progress made in the past months has been achieved by diplomacy backed by a willingness to use military force. It remains critically important, as this process continues, that members of the international community continue to monitor closely the Syrian regime's compliance with its Chemical Weapons Convention (CWC)-related obligations. Syria's obligations are clear, and we will continue to underscore the importance of the Assad regime's continued cooperation. The Security Council decided in UNSCR 2118 to impose Chapter VII measures in the event of noncompliance with the resolution.

While we have made progress, the task before us remains considerable. After months of Syrian foot dragging, we have made clear to the Assad regime that the internationally agreed upon schedule for chemical weapons destruction is simply not up for negotiation; the regime has all the equipment that it needs and has run out of excuses. We remain focused on underscoring the need for Syria to move forward rapidly with transporting chemical weapons materials to the port of Latakia for removal, consistent with its responsibilities under the CWC and UNSCR 2118. The next few weeks are critical in the removal effort, and we and the rest of the world are watching. We have, of course, also been in contact with Syrian opposition leaders, updating them throughout this process, and confirming their commitment that they will not interfere with the activities of the international elimination effort.

With the continuing support of the international community, and the dedicated commitment of the OPCW–UN Joint Mission, we believe the Syrians are capable of completing the removal effort by late April. The international community continues to work toward the June 30th target date for the complete elimination of the program. While Syrian delays have placed that timeline in some danger, we continue to believe they remain achievable.

The path ahead is not an easy one. Syria has missed several intermediate target dates, including most recently the target date for the destruction of chemical weapons production facilities. The regime must meet all chemical weapons destruction obligations, including for the physical destruction of chemical weapons production facilities, consistent with the CWC. The OPCW is currently advising Syria on an appropriate facilities destruction plan. It is essential that Syria accept its recommendations, and submit a revised facilities destruction plan for consideration by the OPCW Executive Council at its next scheduled meeting.

The United States and the international community have provided extensive assistance to the international effort to eliminate the Syrian chemical weapons program. There are no more excuses on the part of the Assad regime for not meeting the agreed timeline. We continue to encourage all countries to make whatever contribution they can to this important undertaking—whether that contribution is financial, technical, or in-kind—to enable the OPCW and U.N. to complete their missions. The United States has led by example in providing tens of millions of dollars in assistance to the OPCW–UN Joint Mission, including the provision of containers, trucks, forklifts, and other materials necessary for the safe transportation of chemical weapons materials in Syria. The State Department's Nonproliferation and Disarmament Fund has provided $8 million in financial and in-kind assistance to the OPCW inspection team, including armored vehicles, training, protective equipment, and medical countermeasures. Most significantly, the United States is also contributing unique capabilities to the elimination effort through the Department of Defense's provision of a U.S. vessel, the Motor Vessel (M/V) *Cape Ray*, equipped with deployable hydrolysis technology to neutralize at sea Syria's highest priority chemical weapons materials (sulfur mustard agent and the sarin precursor chemical, DF).

While U.S. contributions to the elimination efforts are significant, this is ultimately a mission that reflects a remarkable international division of labor. Many of our international partners are participating and providing financial and in-kind assistance that is critical to the effort's success: Danish and Norwegian ships (with Finnish and British support) are removing chemical weapons materials from the Syrian port of Latakia. Russia and China are assisting with security in Syrian territorial waters for the port loading operations. Italy has agreed to provide a port to allow transloading operations from the Danish cargo ship to the *Cape Ray*. The United Kingdom has agreed to destroy nerve agent precursor chemicals through commercial incineration. Germany has agreed to destroy the byproduct resulting from neutralization of the sulfur mustard agent aboard the M/V *Cape Ray* as an in kind contribution. Countries like Japan, Canada, the European Union, and many other states have made generous financial contributions. Companies in the United States and Finland have been awarded contracts from the OPCW for the destruction of the remaining materials.

As the removal and elimination process continues, we will also continue to fully support the OPCW's verification and inspection efforts, to ensure the accuracy and completeness of Syria's declaration. We have never taken the Assad regime at its word, and will continue to press for a robust verification regime to ensure the absence of undeclared materials and facilities. We approach this process with our eyes wide open, and will insist on international verification.

The path ahead will not be smooth, given the unprecedented scope and timeline for the mission. But we remain resolute in addressing these challenges, given the high stakes for the Syrian people, the region, and the world. Thank you again for the opportunity to discuss this important issue with you. I look forward to your questions and to consulting with you closely as we continue our efforts to verifiably eliminate Syria's chemical weapons program.

The CHAIRMAN. Well, thank you both.

It looks like we have not had the second vote yet. So let us start.

Madam Secretary, United States policy on Syria has been premised on the assessment that there is no military solution to end the conflict. However, Assad forces backed, as your own testimony says, by Iran, Russia and Hezbollah have made alarming gains on the ground in recent weeks and likely believe that military victory is possible, as long as United States-backed opposition fighters are mired in a two-front war, fighting al-Qaeda and other Islamic extremists, as well as fighting the regime.

Is the administration considering any military options that could change the calculus of the Assad regime that they cannot win militarily?

Ambassador PATTERSON. Senator, I think that would be better discussed—I mean, we have always said that all options are on the table, but we need to discuss some of these more sensitive issues offline.

The CHAIRMAN. So just the mere fact of answering generically, are you considering any military options, is something that would have to be classified?

Ambassador PATTERSON. Senator, Mr. Chairman——

The CHAIRMAN. I did not get into which ones yet. I just said are there any.

Ambassador PATTERSON. I am not at liberty—first of all, I would not be at liberty to discuss issues that are in a predecisional stage that are under discussion within the administration. And again, they would be of a classified nature. So I would prefer to discuss them with members of this committee in an offline session.

The CHAIRMAN. Well, we are going to, obviously, get to that then.

Let me tell you that I have a problem with a generic answer to a generic question that I cannot believe is classified. I go to these classified hearings, and sometimes I listen to a hearing that in my view should never have been classified because there is nothing there of consequence that I do not read before I get there by the press. Yet, when you go to a classified hearing, of course, you are constrained, but I would not be constrained if what I read in the press is largely what I hear in these hearings. So unless I am going to get something more in these classified settings, you know, that is going to be a problem moving forward.

What is the view of the administration? You mentioned in public testimony that we are helping certain vetted elements of the Syrian opposition. Are we doing enough in this regard? Should we not be doing more? Should we consider what we are doing in terms of the weapons that we give them in order to be able to truly change the calculus? If you cannot stop a helicopter or a plane that is bombing you, if you cannot stop a tank that is crushing your community, then I do not know how we ever change the calculus here.

Ambassador PATTERSON. Mr. Chairman, absolutely we are not doing enough to help the moderate opposition, and our deliveries certainly of nonlethal equipment have been stymied by a series of logistical issues and security issues that have taken place both in Turkey and over the border in Syria because it has been at times very difficult to deliver this equipment. We are trying to change our strategy. We have changed our strategy, at least for one shipment, and delivered medical supplies on February 20 to vetted units, to trusted commanders that we have worked with very specifically. So we were trying to get more equipment to these commanders—get it more rapidly.

And importantly I think we are starting to pay people and municipalities so that will provide some pushback, some counteraction to the ability of extremist groups to pay young Syrian men to join their ranks. We are trying to support communities more actively. We have spent over $60 million in supporting communities. But, no, of course, we have not done enough to support the moderate opposition.

The CHAIRMAN. Well, Okay. But medical supplies—I am all for it. We obviously have to help those who are wounded in the fight, but that does not help you stop a tank. It does not help you stop a plane. It does not help you stop a helicopter that is barrel bombing you.

Ambassador PATTERSON. Mr. Chairman, I think you would find great unanimity within the administration that what you say is accurate, that they need more support of all sorts. And again, I would prefer to discuss that with you or your staff in a more private setting.

The CHAIRMAN. Let me go to an area that hopefully you can answer in public. U.N. Special Envoy Brahimi this week suggested that proceeding with elections in Syria would end the Geneva II process. Is this also the administration's position? What are the prospects that the elections will take place this spring, that Assad will run, that he will win, and what is the consequence of that to any negotiation?

Ambassador PATTERSON. Well, the consequence is, I think, that these elections will be internally illegitimate. Syria does not exactly have a history of free and fair elections. You cannot hold an election with 9 million or 10 million people outside the country and where much of the country is cut off so that people could not vote freely even if they were so inclined. And I think there will be virtually universal recognition of this by the international community.

The Geneva II process has faltered, but in our view it is an important element to keep alive because at some point, if the calculus or the balance on the battlefield changes, you need essentially to have a process that people can resort to.

The CHAIRMAN. Let me ask Secretary Countryman. I heard your remarks about the chemical weapons which I believe—the process of eliminating Syria's chemical weapons was made possible by this committee's bipartisan vote for the authorization for the use of force for the President, as he was headed to the G20 in Russia. But as you yourself acknowledge, Syria's 12 chemical weapons production facilities were to be destroyed by March 15. They have failed to meet this deadline as well, now offering to seal off these facilities instead of destroying them.

What is the U.S. Government prepared to do to ensure that Syria complies with the Chemical Weapons Convention and what is the likelihood of Syria's entire chemical arsenal being destroyed by June the 30th?

Mr. COUNTRYMAN. First, Mr. Chairman, I agree with you that the agreement for the elimination of Syria's chemical weapons was achieved only by using a credible threat of force. And I greatly value this committee's role in adding to the credibility of that threat.

In terms of physical production facilities, the equipment that has been declared has been destroyed. The facilities themselves, whether they are buildings, tunnels, or hangars, still remains to be destroyed. We have maintained and will continue to maintain that destruction means destruction. I think there will be further action in the OPCW Executive Council in the next week that will address this question. So I am not quite prepared to predict that it will be immediately successful, but I can guarantee you of our firm stand on this issue.

In terms of estimating the likelihood of the complete elimination of Syria's program, we are focused at the moment—that is, the international community—on the removal and destruction of declared chemicals, and I believe that we can still achieve the target date of mid-2014 for that destruction.

The question of whether the declaration is accurate is, as I indicated, the next question that we will have to take up.

The CHAIRMAN. And I want to go to Senator Corker, so he can get his questions in before we have to go to vote.

But let me just say what is the consequence if June 30 comes and goes and we are nowhere near to achieving what we set out to achieve and which the Syrians agreed to.

Mr. COUNTRYMAN. Very briefly, I would differentiate two situations.

If by June 30 we have removed all declared chemicals from Syria and they are aboard the U.S. vessel that is in the process of destroying those chemicals, I think that we will be successful. And I do not know of anyone in the world who would criticize us for not completing the destruction process 100 percent when we have eliminated those chemicals from the possibility of their use by the regime.

If alternately Syria does not complete the removal process of declared chemicals by that date, it is a very different situation and one that will have strong consequences for Syria.

The CHAIRMAN. Okay. I still have not heard what they are, but Senator Corker.

Senator CORKER. Thank you, Mr. Chairman.

Before I begin, I want to say to Ambassador Patterson that, look, I respect you tremendously and have spent a lot of time with you in Pakistan and Egypt. And I would imagine being in a position you are in right now where you are having to talk in this manner relative to Syria is very uncomfortable. Again, I want to say I have tremendous respect for you.

I find the answer that you gave relative to the classified setting and potential military efforts major baloney, and if I was in a different setting, I would use different words. I cannot imagine you saying that in this setting. That would indicate to people that we actually have a military strategy relative to Syria, and that could not be further from the truth.

Now, are you sitting here trying to indicate to the media and people listening that you guys have actually developed a military strategy relative to Syria and you are going to talk about it in a classified setting? Is that what you are doing today? Because if you are, that is major news. And I find that answer—a friend, someone I respect—to be one of the most major misleading baloneys I have heard since I have been in the United States Senate. So please clarify that because I am pretty upset, especially after we wrote an authorization for the use of force and this administration did everything they could to keep from doing that, jumping in the arms of Russia, basically validating Assad through this shiny object issue of chemical warfare being removed from the country, which has nothing to do with the 40,000 people that have been killed since August with barrel bombs. So please clarify what you said.

Ambassador PATTERSON. Yes. Senator Corker, I am sorry if it sounds like baloney, but let me do try and clarify this because perhaps I interpreted Senator Menendez's question too narrowly. Obviously, our view and often state view is there is no military solution to this conflict.

Senator CORKER. And there is no military strategy the administration has laid out.

Ambassador PATTERSON. Wait a minute, sir. Wait just a sec. Let me get to that.

So there is no military solution, and there has to be a negotiated settlement.

I thought what Senator Menendez was asking me is were military options under consideration, and no, I am simply not going to get to that in this kind of hearing.

Senator CORKER. Are you going to indicate in this public hearing that you are actually considering military options—this administration?

Ambassador PATTERSON. Senator, I am not going to get into that and I am not going to be, in effect, bullied into answering this with all due respect, sir.

Senator CORKER. Well, let me explain to the world I assure you the administration has no military options on the table.

And I would just like to ask you what is our strategy. I mean, sending in—you know, I sat with Idris last August while he was waiting on the trucks to arrive that had been promised for months. He is obviously not a part of this anymore. But what is our strategy in Syria? I do not see that we have one other than letting people kill each other off, allowing it to fester.

Ambassador PATTERSON. Senator, I do think we have a strategy.

Senator CORKER. Please lay it out one, two, three.

Ambassador PATTERSON. Let me try and lay out the components of the strategy because I do think we have a strategy here.

One is diplomatic and that is not zero. We do have——

Senator CORKER. Wait a minute.

Ambassador PATTERSON. Wait a minute.

Senator CORKER. It is pretty zero.

Ambassador PATTERSON. Pretty zero, but——

Senator CORKER. Okay. You did say just now ''pretty zero.'' So that is pretty zero.

What is the next strategy?

Ambassador PATTERSON. The next strategy is containment, and we are working with our allies——

Senator CORKER. So we are going to contain all the jihadists there and get everybody killed off?

Ambassador PATTERSON. We are going to work with our allies, Senator Corker, to try and improve their border security, to try and improve their security, and in other things again I will not mention in this classified hearing, to try and help our allies out with both security assistance and humanitarian assistance.

Senator CORKER. And our allies are who again?

Ambassador PATTERSON. Well, our friends are Jordan in particular, Lebanon——

Senator CORKER. And Jordan is inside fighting? I mean, I am missing something here.

Ambassador PATTERSON. Jordanians inside——

Senator CORKER. So I am talking about inside Syria. I understand about the refugee camps and I understand all those things. But inside Syria, what is our strategy? I understand that we are trying to keep Jordan stable because we do not have a serious strategy and we have people coming into Jordan and that is destabilizing the country. I got that. But what are we doing as far as a Syrian strategy goes?

Ambassador PATTERSON. We are trying to support the moderate opposition, and I would——

Senator CORKER. Support them how? With food and——

Ambassador PATTERSON. With food and with other goods and with supplies. And again, let us not get into some of these other things here.

Senator CORKER. Can we have a classified setting immediately after this? I mean, would you be open to that, going down to SVC–215 and let us just hear some of these details that would be worth our while to do?

Ambassador PATTERSON. Well, we will talk about it. I mean, I would certainly be willing.

But let me go on. Senator Corker, we do have a counterterrorism strategy. There is a huge amount of intelligence exchange and working with intelligence agencies in the region to get a handle on these jihadis who have migrated from all over the world. So we are trying to——

Senator CORKER. So we are getting intelligence on all these jihadis that are flowing in from everywhere that has created a significant threat to the homeland, but we are gathering intelligence. What is the next element of that?

Ambassador PATTERSON. Well, the next step, Senator Corker, will be to work with our allies, work with our friends in the region to try and reduce this threat.

Senator CORKER. We have no strategy in Syria. We have not had a strategy in Syria from day one.

And I guess I would ask you what is our relationship, for instance, with Russia and Iran and the other things that we have ongoing with them. How is that affecting the fact that we have no strategy, no coherent strategy in Syria whatsoever? I mean, I would feel better about it if you would just say that to me. We have no strategy. But to act like we have got some classified strategy we are going to hear about, I am looking forward to that meeting. But does our relationship with Russia and Iran have something to do with our lack of strategy in Syria?

Ambassador PATTERSON. Senator, we work closely—certainly Secretary Kerry and everybody else who is involved has worked closely with the Russians particularly to try and get them to cooperate with us in the diplomatic process. It is a process that has largely failed. We have, I think, been successful with the Russians in cooperating on the removal of the chemical weapons, and we are hopeful that we can engage with them as this process goes forward because a destabilized Syria is not just a threat to us and neighbors, but it is also a threat to Russia.

Senator CORKER. If I could just say one last thing. And I know I do not usually show much emotions in these meetings, especially to someone who I respect so much and I have to believe has been put in an incredibly awkward position being here today.

But, Mr. Countryman, I will say to you this removal of chemical weapons—I would say the reason Assad is dragging his feet, as he is, is that is the very thing that has validated him. It is the thing that we did to put him in the strongest position he has been in since this conflict began. And the reason he is dragging his feet is, as long as he is important to that process, he is going to continue to be buoyed up. And I think it is a shiny object; 1,200 people were killed terribly with chemical weapons; 40,000 people have been killed since then with barrel bombs. And to me the whole issue regarding the chemical weapons has been a ruse. It has been a shiny object. It has kept us from really having any kind of coherent Syrian policy in the beginning.

And I am not blaming our country for what has happened in Syria. I mean, it is something we did not create. But to act like we have some policy that is going to solve this problem when we cannot even get trucks delivered to the head of the opposition on the ground in an appropriate amount of time because of the bureaucratic tape that we have here in this country and the fact that we really have no commitment to me is very disappointing.

So I find this portion of our hearing incredibly disappointing. I hope that we will never have another hearing like this with you, Ambassador. I still call you that because of my great respect. And I do look forward to that classified briefing in just a moment that is going to be so illuminating on this new Syrian strategy.

Mr. COUNTRYMAN. Senator, if I could very briefly disagree with you with great respect.

First, I do not agree at all that the agreement to rid Syria of its chemical weapons has either validated or strengthened the Assad regime.

Senator CORKER. Has he been strengthened since we began this the 1st of September?

Mr. COUNTRYMAN. Since September, yes, but the question of cause and effect of whether the chemical weapons agreement, which forced him to give up what he considered his most valued strategic deterrent against Israel, which he had used in a tactical sense against his own people and which he is now constrained from using—these are actual security losses for him. And no amount of Russian praise for his so-called wise decision can allow him to regain the credibility that he frittered away, that he destroyed with his own people and with the international community. And it does not change in any way the United States view that he needs to go if Syria is to have a chance.

Senator CORKER. Well, with great respect, the best thing that ever happened to Assad—this sounds really crass. The best thing he ever did was kill 1,200 citizens with chemical weapons because the United States and Russia and others have now propped him up and used that 1,200-person killing to allow 40,000 more people to be killed. And it is a shiny object. It was a great way for us to partner with Russia and move away from having any kind of strategy on the ground. So I disagree with you strongly. With respect, I think you are delusional.

Mr. COUNTRYMAN. If I could expand on my delusions, I would simply say that chemical weapons were never an important part of the military equation causing the tragedy in Syria, and their elimination does not fundamentally alter the military equation that causes today's situation.

The CHAIRMAN. I will say I understand the ranking member's frustration on the broader question, and I share it with him. I will disagree with him on the chemical weapons insofar as it was important to send not only in Syria but internationally a message that the use of chemical weapons against all international norms would have a consequence. And that is where I would have a difference of opinion, but I strongly respect his overall frustration with where we are at on Syria.

Senator Kaine has been gracious enough to come back, and he has his own questions. I am going to ask him to preside. I am going to go vote. I am going to come back. There are a couple more questions and a preface that I want to set for that classified setting so that it can actually be useful at the end of the day because if we cannot meet the standard that I will ask you to meet, then we might as well not have it. I will be right back.

Senator KAINE [presiding]. Thank you, Mr. Chairman. Thanks to the witnesses. And I apologize for being tardy. We are ''backing and forthing'' on votes.

By way of comment, strategy conveys a lot of different things. Let us just talk about humanitarian efforts. The United States is the largest provider of humanitarian relief in the world. That is not by accident. It is strategic. That is an important thing. I just returned from visiting Lebanon, and the United States support for humanitarian relief for Syrian refugees outside the borders of Syria is highly appreciated. We need to do more. We need the other nations to do more. But that is an element of strategy. We want to do more with humanitarian relief inside Syria.

Let me ask a question of both of you. Since the U.N. Security Council Resolution 2139, there is a 30-day reporting requirement. What do you expect to see in the opening 30 days? I am gathering it is not going to be too good. What do you expect to see in the opening 30-day report of the U.N. Security Resolution 2139?

Ambassador PATTERSON. Thank you, Senator Kaine.

We do not expect to see very much. It has been very hard to implement the resolution and move the humanitarian goods across the border. There have been some desultory meetings and there has been a plan developed, but in terms of actual delivery to hungry people, there has been very little. So we anticipate that that will be the report that is given from the international relief agencies. We have been working with the opposition, of course, to ensure that assistance can get into opposition-held areas.

Senator KAINE. I am going to introduce a statement to the record from Mercy Corps outlining some ideas about humanitarian relief. There is no one here to object to my request, so without objection, it will be entered into the record.

[The information referred to can be found on page 83.]

Senator KAINE. The issue of aggressive insertion of humanitarian aid into the country is a huge and important one. In Turkey, Jordan, and Lebanon now, we have heard thank you for the United States work on humanitarian aid outside. What we need now is humanitarian aid inside. That continues to remain an important area for us to focus on.

The second element of strategy is diplomacy. I share Ambassador Countryman's view that the destruction of one of the largest chemical weapons stockpiles in the world is a very significant diplomatic achievement. We are not happy with what is going on in Syria. We are not happy with the progress. We are not happy with the civil war and the slaughter of innocent people. However, the existence of that chemical weapons stockpile would be bad for Syrians today and would be bad for Syrians and all neighbors tomorrow and for years to come. That destruction is a significant diplomatic gain.

What is the current status of the destruction of the chemical weapons stockpile? We have seen some positive news. We have seen some negative news. In particular, with respect to the announced June 30 deadline for destruction, how is it looking?

Mr. COUNTRYMAN. In brief—I cover more of this in my written statement, but to summarize, nearly half of the chemicals that Syria has declared have been unloaded through the Port of Latakia onto a Danish vessel. When the loading is complete, they will be transferred to a U.S. vessel for destruction. Almost half sounds good. One of the things that concerns us is that 65 percent of the more dangerous chemicals, the Priority 1 chemicals, have yet to be moved out of Syria. The pace has increased dramatically in the last 3 weeks, and we have solid grounds to believe it can be accomplished in April—100 percent removal. But we need to keep our elbow in the back of the Syrians with the help of the joint mission of the U.N., the OPCW, and the international community. Once it is all loaded onto the U.S. ship for destruction, we believe that we will either meet or come very close to the June 30 target date for destruction of declared chemicals.

Senator KAINE. And then let me ask about declared. What is our assessment of whether the declaration of chemical weapons—how close does it match reality, and are there significant questions we have about the extent of the declaration whether there are undeclared weapons we need to isolate and identify?

Mr. COUNTRYMAN. Having great concern for the frustration that the chairman has already expressed, I can only offer to brief you on that in a closed session.

Senator KAINE. Well, that is a question that is very important for us to know.

Mr. COUNTRYMAN. It will be illuminating.

Senator KAINE. Okay, thank you.

So diplomacy is an element of strategy. Chemical weapons we have discussed.

The second element of diplomacy is the talks in Geneva. Those are desultory. They are not achieving what we hope. But we do know if we do not continue talking, we know what the answer will be. There will not be the negotiated political end to this civil war that we all think is necessary. So we have to undertake continuing efforts to engage the parties in dialogue.

The third element of strategy is obviously military. That is probably the area that has excited the frustration I was hearing as I came in the door, and that is one, look, we can all share. We were around this table together—members of the Foreign Relations Committee—voting for a request for limited military action in Syria. It was essentially a 10–8 vote, very divided, not a partisan division, but very divided. Most would acknowledge that Congress was not going to support that. Certainly the House was not going to. It would have been very difficult for the Senate to support it. So it is understandably frustrating if you think the United States should have a clear military policy as a third element of strategy. Congress has pretty much spoken that they were not in support of military action even for the limited use of deterring and degrading the capacity to use chemical weapons. So if we are going to be frustrated, we can be frustrated, but it should not be just why is the administration not doing better when Congress had a chance to vote and express their support or lack of support for military option and pretty much said they did not support it. So we can all be frustrated by that.

But I will leave questions about the military discussion for a closed session.

Let us go to the refugee crisis in the neighboring countries. Clearly, Jordan, Turkey, as recent events have shown with the shooting down of the Syrian aircraft, Lebanon where I recently visited—I feel like the Lebanese story has sort of been an undertold story and the effect of the refugees on Lebanese life, about 4 million Lebanese, over a million Syrian refugees in Lebanon. The Syrian civil war is the dark star of gravity that is altering every fact of Lebanese life, economy, education, tourism, extremist violence perpetrated against largely Shia sites because of Hezbollah's decision to go into all-in for Assad in Syria.

What more can we be doing to help our allies and countries that are neighboring countries? I failed to mention Iraq, but the challenges are significant there. What more can we be doing to help these countries who are allies of ours deal with these refugee flows, which are continuing?

Ambassador PATTERSON. Yes, Senator Kaine. I think the Lebanon story is sort of underplayed in this narrative because they certainly have the most refugees, and they are in host communities, which means local municipalities are bearing the burden. We need to step up humanitarian assistance particularly in Lebanon and Jordan where the situation is acute.

And in Iraq, in particular, where the security implications have really been more severe than the refugee flow, we have tried and again need to do more to accelerate shipments of military equipment to Iraqi forces. And we have begun to train Iraqi special forces again in Jordan. So we are trying to help the Iraqi Government meet the spillover effect—counter the spillover effect from the Syrian crisis.

So a combination I think of security assistance—certainly we are upping that to Lebanon this year. We are upping our assistance to Jordan and increased humanitarian assistance. We are very mindful of the challenges that that presents to the neighbors.

Senator KAINE. I am going to ask—Senator Coons will now take questions. I will go cast a vote and return.

Senator COONS [presiding]. Thank you, Senator Kaine.

If I could first, before welcoming our witnesses, I just want to thank Chairman Menendez for chairing this important hearing and our witnesses for sharing their insights into what is an ongoing crisis.

I joined my colleagues, including Chairman Menendez, Ranking Member Corker, in sending a letter to the President expressing bipartisan support for seeking a new strategy that will break the stalemate on the ground and enable a meaningful political solution that paves a new way for leadership in Syria. In my view, we cannot afford to sit on the sidelines as innocent civilians are killed and have to take steps to diminish the huge amount of suffering that has already happened in Syria while preventing the establishment of safe havens for al-Qaeda-related extremists. And I believe we need to recalibrate our policy in Syria.

We have met a number of times, Madam Assistant Secretary, and I have always been impressed with your leadership, your insight, and your capabilities, especially in this most difficult of fields.

So if you will forgive me for a moment, given that I have literally just returned from casting a vote. I was particularly interested in the impact of refugees on host countries in the region and in particular what you thought are the potential challenges for our most vital ally Jordan and other allies in the region. Forgive me if this has already been addressed.

Ambassador PATTERSON. Thank you, Senator Coons.

I know that many of you spoke to King Abdullah when he was here, and he was extremely eloquent about the challenges that Jordan is facing in this respect, not only in the refugee camp, which can become certainly a hot bed of its own resentments and insurgency, frankly, but also in the host communities because it has put a huge burden on Jordanian public services, as well as in Lebanon and elsewhere in the region.

So in Jordan, in particular, we are increasing our humanitarian assistance. We are increasing our economic assistance, and we are increasing our assistance to Jordanian military and security forces, including on the border so they have a better capacity to patrol the border and prevent spillover, in effect, and also to train their irregular forces in a more aggressive way.

In Lebanon, we are going to increase security assistance there as well. That really in numbers the most severely affected country. Trying to increase our humanitarian assistance there. In Lebanon, they are entirely in host communities. So it has put an enormous burden on the local population.

Senator COONS. I have previously met with the Ambassadors from both Jordan and Lebanon in my Appropriations Committee role and was struck both at their gratitude for and their intense need for additional humanitarian assistance from the United States.

I visited last year a Syrian refugee camp in Jordan, and the refugees expressed extreme frustration and anger at delays in the promised delivery of U.S. assistance and support.

What can we do to express in any meaningful way a sense of abandonment by the United States felt by Syrians within the country and in the region? And how has that, in your view, manifested itself in terms of radicalization of the opposition forces?

Ambassador PATTERSON. Well, I think one huge attraction to the opposition forces inside of Syria or the more extremist elements of the opposition forces is they pay money. They essentially pay salaries. So as I mentioned earlier, we are going to try and counteract that, at least within Syria, to try and pay police, sanitation workers, teachers, taxi, deliverer of public services and provide some balance to that respect.

In the camps, Senator Coons, I think perhaps we have not done a very good job of identifying where the assistance comes from. Most of our assistance in these camps is channeled through very worthy international organizations, but sometimes the sources of funds is a little obscure, at least to the recipient. And we need to do a better job of articulating that because we are by far the largest donor and frankly a donor that delivers on our promises, unlike some of the others. But I must say the international community has been responsive in great measure to this crisis.

Senator COONS. What more can we do to ensure that the assistance that we are providing goes to the intended beneficiaries and through channels that we expect, particularly with regard to lethal aid?

Ambassador PATTERSON. Well, we are handling nonlethal, Senator Coons, and there were some issues with that in December where a warehouse was overrun by other elements. But now we are sending materials directly to trusted commanders, and the SMC has been very helpful in that respect because they have helped us identify commanders in whom they have confidence. So we are delivering goods directly to them, vetted commanders.

Senator COONS. I am also, before I turn it over to another Senator, particularly interested in the progress toward the chemical weapons commitments that were made. How likely is it in your view that Syria will meet the June deadline for the removal and destruction of much of the chemical weapons stockpile? If Secretary Countryman would like to speak to that. Forgive me.

Mr. COUNTRYMAN. Thank you, Senator.

We believe that there are no obstacles to completing the removal of the declared stockpile from Syria in the month of April, and it will require constant attention from the international community to make sure that happens. Assuming for a moment that it happens, we will be either on time or very close to on time to completing the destruction of those chemicals aboard the U.S.-outfitted ship. But the key point is that the most dangerous chemicals, those that the regime has used against its people, will be out of the hands of the regime well before June.

Senator COONS. Last, if I could, as you go through a review, what do you think should be the overarching goal of United States policy toward Syria, and how do we execute on that? If you would both answer that, and then I will——

Ambassador PATTERSON. Senator, the overarching goal at this point is to change the calculus on the battlefield so that the Assad regime has an incentive to negotiate, and we have not yet reached that point.

The other, frankly, extreme concern of the administration is the growing terrorist threat emanating from Syria not just with individuals, although that is severe enough, but the possible establishment of a safe haven, semipermanent safe haven, in northeastern Syria.

And those are two issues that need to be addressed urgently.

Senator COONS. I agree with the urgency.

Mr. Assistant Secretary.

Mr. COUNTRYMAN. Nothing to add, sir.

Senator COONS. Great. Thank you both. I appreciate your testimony.

Senator McCain.

Senator McCAIN. Well, thank you, Senator.

I thank the witnesses.

So if I heard you right, we are going to change the calculus on the battlefield. Is that one of our policy goals?

Ambassador PATTERSON. Our policy goal, Senator, is to move toward a negotiated settlement.

Senator MCCAIN. Can that happen without changing the calculus on the battlefield?

Ambassador PATTERSON. Oh, of course, we will have to change the calculus on the battlefield because——

Senator MCCAIN. Thank you. We once had the calculus on the battlefield about 2 years ago before Hezbollah, Russian arms, Iranian Revolutionary Guard, and others.

So tell me when I am wrong here. The Geneva gathering was a total and abysmal failure. The only concrete thing I have seen out of Geneva is that the families of the people who went there have been kidnapped by Bashar al-Assad. So they have paid a pretty heavy price to go to Geneva, as nice as it must have been that time of year.

Syria-Iraq border is now a haven for al-Qaeda where they are moving back and forth.

The weapons from Russia continue to flow in even according to a story I have here that they have even increased their arms supplies. Please correct me if I am wrong.

Robert Ford, the former Ambassador to Syria, America alone cannot solve the Syrian crisis.

We now see a front page story this morning about the fact that the Syrian resistance are now giving up because of the failure to achieve success where they now have a program to amnesty for these people supposedly.

Maybe you can help me out here. How is that policy that you just articulated—how is that doing?

Ambassador PATTERSON. Not very well, Senator.

Senator MCCAIN. Not very well.

Ambassador PATTERSON. And I said that sort of front-up, right up front. Can I address the points you raised?

Senator MCCAIN. Sure.

Ambassador PATTERSON. Look, on the Geneva process, I think we totally admit that these talks have faltered, and there is no process underway right now.

But I think if you talk, Senator, to members of the opposition, first of all, it is sort of to unify the opposition and give them more credibility within Syria. And I think if you talk to them—and we are hoping they can come here soon—I do not think they would say that they were sorry they went, despite the enormous personal cost that some of them have endured, because it was a process that gave them legitimacy and also exposed the regime on the international stage.

On the Syria-Iraq border, Senator——

Senator MCCAIN. Let me just respond to that assertion. So really, the purpose of Geneva was not to arrange the transition out of power of Assad. It was to give the opposition more legitimacy even though many of them had their family members kidnapped by Assad. I got that. Okay.

What is the next point?

Ambassador PATTERSON. Senator, that is not right.

Senator MCCAIN. It was a failure. It was a failure and it was doomed to failure because we knew that without the battlefield favoring Bashar al-Assad, he was not going to negotiate his departure. A first-year cadet at West Point knows that, Madam Secretary, that when they are winning on the battlefield, which Bashar al-Assad is, he is not going to negotiate his transition from power. So it was all Assad and a joke. Now, whether it helped some with the legitimacy of the opposition or not, I mean, that is a reason to have gone to Geneva?

Go ahead.

Ambassador PATTERSON. Again, Senator, I think you should, as we have and you will soon I am sure, talk to some of these individuals.

Senator MCCAIN. I have talked to them, by the way.

Ambassador PATTERSON. I know. Okay.

Senator MCCAIN. I have talked to them. Please. I have been in Syria, ma'am.

Ambassador PATTERSON. I know, Senator.

And I would agree with you about the Syria-Iraq border. That border is beginning to disappear because of the presence of insurgence and extremists on both sides of the border.

There is a constant flow of arms from Russia. I believe that they probably have increased recently. But it has been constant over quite a long period of time.

I think you are referring to the article in the ''Wall Street Journal'' today about the cease-fires. The battlefield situation ebbs and flows, but yes, these are basically areas that have been defeated by the regime and basically develop a temporary cease-fire so food and supplies can get in.

So I, frankly, would agree with much of what you said.

Senator MCCAIN. Well, you know the sad part about all this, Madam Secretary, is that those of us who observed Syria and saw what was happening there and said we must help these people and watched the 5,000 Hezbollah come in at the demand of Iran and watched the increased arms flows from Russia while we trumpeted the fact that we were arranging for the departure of the chemical weapons after, of course, we said we were going to strike them and did not, which reverberated around the world and still does—and we watched the slaughter take place and we knew what they needed. And they needed antitank and antiair capability even though there is always a risk with any weapons you give them. And we watched Bashar al-Assad succeed and consolidate his power.

Meanwhile, it went from basically a civil war to now what is a regional conflict, destabilizing the neighbors, mass exoduses of refugees, and we decided the policy of this Government and this President was basically to do nothing. In fact, I remember it was said, well, we are keeping Iran pinned down. And the slaughter goes on—150,000 people.

So our redline—it was not any of this, but the redline was that if Bashar al-Assad used chemical weapons, we would strike. So the President of the United States, I guess, according to media reports, took a walk and then came back and said, well, we are going to have to go to Congress, knowing full well that Congress would not agree. He never made the case to the Congress and the American people.

So sometimes I apologize for getting a little emotional about this. This is a colossal failure of American ability to help people who are struggling for freedom. It is a colossal failure.

Again, I guess what you just said is really the best example I can think of of the way we just practice this foolishness. The reason why Geneva was a success is because it gave legitimacy to the opposition who got their family members kidnapped? You know, it was advertised as a way to arrange Bashar al-Assad's departure from power, and anybody knew that as long as Bashar al-Assad was winning, they would not agree to transition from power.

So, you know, it is really one of the great tragedies of the 21st century and maybe even in some ways the 20th. While the greatest nation in the world sat by and watched this genocide taking place and the spread of it and these thousands of al-Qaedas who will now, after this conflict is over or maybe before, go back to the countries they came from and practice the things they have learned, and we will again have sat by and watched.

And no one that I know of wanted American boots on the ground. That is the favorite administration response. Well, I guess they want American boots on the ground. No, we never said that. We wanted to give them what they needed to defend themselves and win, which they were doing 2 years ago.

So I thank you for your service. You and I have known each other for many, many years, but I have to be honest with you. You are here defending the indefensible and you still have not articulated a policy that the United States of America has.

I thank you, Mr. Chairman.

I am glad to hear a response if you want to.

Senator COONS. If I might, Madam Secretary, by way of inviting that response, you agree with some of the factual predicates Senator McCain laid out about what has happened. In your opening statement, you suggested we are reviewing our policy and identifying priorities for coordinated action. Given where we are, how do you believe we can change the dynamics on the battlefield and lay the groundwork for a better path forward?

Ambassador PATTERSON. Thank you, Senator Coons.

And let me try and answer that, Senator McCain, because of course, I disagree that we do not have a policy. I would agree that many elements of our policy have not been successful, and I would also agree with you that the results on the ground are extremely distressing and of enormous long-term concern.

But I think we are trying to revise our policy now. We are trying to accelerate equipment and goods to the opposition. We are trying to step up security assistance to the neighbors to allow them to better defend themselves against the spillover. We are trying to step up the humanitarian assistance elements of this. And we do have a diplomatic strategy that is not solely related to Geneva II. With the Contact Group and the international allies, we are working very closely on the CT area, in the counterterrorism area, with the other countries and intelligence-sharing. So we are trying to change the policy to address some of these issues that you so very eloquently laid out.

Senator MCCAIN. Well, I thank you. I guess my only response is facts are stubborn things. This conflict has been going on for over 3 years, 150,000 people dead, and we are now revising our policy.

The CHAIRMAN [presiding]. Well, seeing no other member, here is the following thing. I think we want to get to the heart of the information, and so an immediate briefing I do not think would produce what the ranking member and I want to hear. So the ranking member and I have agreed to the following. We will have a classified hearing. Here is what we expect, and if you cannot do this, then let us know so none of us are wasting our time.

Number one, what are all the military options being considered, and whether or not they have been chosen as it relates to assisting the vetted Syrian rebels inside of Syria?

Two, what are all the actions, overt and covert, being taken at this time with elements of the vetted Syrian rebels?

Three, what happens to undisclosed elements of chemical weapons that we may subsequently become aware of?

Four, what is the consequence of Syria not meeting its obligations under the agreement to remove all of its—to destroy all of its chemical weapons by June the 30th?

So that is what we want to know. I do not want to go to a classified hearing with what I read in the New York Times. If you cannot do that—and I want anyone and everyone who is in a capacity and at a level to answer those questions. Now, that may be you, Ambassador, which is fine. But I do not want to hear that it is somebody else. I want whomever is necessary to answer all of those questions.

Senator Corker, is there anything you wanted to——

Senator CORKER. I think I was listening closely, and I like everything that you have said. I would like to end this hearing [in a classified session], if it occurs, hearing of every degree of assistance that we are giving the opposition. I want to hear every cell, decimal point. I want to hear every description of what we may or may not being doing relative to the opposition.

And I want to say in my earlier comments my staff is a little concerned about one statement I made relative to Assad. My point is that from the standpoint of him being where he is today strategically, what he did with the chemical weapons while crass, while something that violates every international norm that we have, the way we have responded to that or the way we responded to him doing that has validated his position, caused him to be stronger, and actually caused him to garner support and be in a position where he is actually looking now at running for President again this summer. And that is my point relative to him strategically from his own survival standpoint making a decision that from his own survival standpoint was the smartest thing he possibly could have done because of the way we have responded and the fact that we have no strategy. We have done nothing to change the balance on the ground, nothing whatsoever. And in the interim, he has become validated in the process.

So I thank you for that. I thank you for having this hearing. I am looking forward to this classified setting where, quote, all of this new information is going to be coming forth.

The CHAIRMAN. And I would add one final thing for that setting, although I do not really think it is necessary for that setting, but in order to get the fullness of the answer, I want to know what role do we think that Russia and Iran, if any, will play as it relates to changing the dynamic in Syria.

Ambassador PATTERSON. I am sorry, sir?

The CHAIRMAN. I want to know what role, if any, do we think that Russia and Iran might play in changing the dynamic is Syria.

Okay. With the thanks of—Senator Murphy, do you have a question for this panel? I was just about to excuse them.

Senator MURPHY. No.

The CHAIRMAN. With the thanks of the committee, we look forward to seeing you in a classified setting.

Ambassador PATTERSON. Thank you, sir. Thank you, Mr. Chairman.

The CHAIRMAN. Let me call up our second panel: Dr. David Kilcullen, Chairman and Founder of Caerus Associates; Dr. Vali Nasr, Dean of the Johns Hopkins School for Advanced International Studies; and Jan Egeland, the Secretary General of the Norwegian Refugee Council. We invite our panelists to come on up.

As I said to our previous panel, your full statements will be included in the record, without objection.

I would ask you to summarize them in around 5 minutes or so so that we can enter into a dialogue with you. As a very prestigious panel, I think you can provide a lot of insights to us, and we look forward to your testimony.

Dr. Kilcullen, we will start with you and then Dr. Nasr and then Mr. Egeland.

STATEMENT OF DR. DAVID J. KILCULLEN, CHAIRMAN AND FOUNDER, CAERUS ASSOCIATES, WASHINGTON, DC

Dr. KILCULLEN. Senator Menendez, Senator Corker, members of the committee, thank you for the opportunity to testify on this very important but also, as we have just seen, very controversial issue about options post-Geneva II for United States policy in Syria.

I am going to confine my remarks primarily to things that have not already been discussed in detail, if that is okay. I agree with many of the factual points put forward by both the previous panel and the members of the committee in the discussion. We can elaborate some of those issues if you would like to.

I would slightly differ with the point of view that the regime is winning the conflict on the ground. So with your permission, I will just talk a little about that.

The regime at this point does not entirely control any city with the exception of downtown Damascus. In every other major population center, it has either been replaced by rebel governance structures or it is heavily contested by rural guerillas and urban resisters. And in fact, the Syrian countryside and smaller towns are very heavily contested, and even in formerly regime-controlled areas, we see significant opposition to the regime from the community.

At this point, the regime has lost control of roughly 75 percent of Syrian territory, and although rebel groups had fractured along ideological and sectarian lines in the past, in the last 4 months, we have actually started to see a drop in that degree of fragmentation.

We have seen greater unity emerging within the opposition. We have seen, for example, the formation of the Islamic Front, which is comprised of seven Islamist factions that are working together, and the Southern Front, which just emerged several weeks ago, which has almost 50 more moderate factions working together. And as a result, even though the regime has mounted some relatively successful military operations in the last couple of months, we have actually seen three separate and actually quite successful rebel operations against the regime in the same time.

In general terms, I do not think that the regime is winning. I think that we are in what I would call an escalating stalemate. The conflict is getting more violent. It is not static. The degree of violence is ratcheting up, but at this point neither the rebels nor the regime is in a position to achieve outright military victory. And agreeing with former speakers on the panel, I think that that is, in fact, the key problem, that neither side at this point can actually win militarily but both sides, particularly the regime, still think that they can. And that has resulted in a fairly significant surge of violence this spring.

So the regime's Qalamoun offensive, which I know you have been referring to indirectly, is focused on cementing control, although a very narrow triangle of territory from Aleppo in the north to Damascus in the south, and then west to the coast. And since January, government forces have, indeed, captured the town of Yabroud on the Lebanese border. They have advanced west of Homs. They have captured Krak des Chevaliers, the old crusader castle. They have killed a very large number of rebels recently in Ghouta, which is the same part to the east of Damascus where the chemical attack happened last August. So they have made some military progress on the ground.

They have also consolidated the various nonprofessional irregular military groups that were working, known sometimes as shabiha, thugs, or ghosts, to oppress the population. They have consolidated them into the national defense forces, a force of about 60,000 fighters, which has become very important to them in holding ground. So there is some progress on the regime side.

But just in the last month, insurgents seized districts on the north and east of Aleppo. They have increased their control in Aleppo province and in Idlib province. They have now cut off a very substantial number of regime outposts in the north. And in the northeast, a separate rebel offensive has been clearing regime positions in Deir ez Zor and along the Euphrates River, and a third offensive in the south mounted by the Southern Front has expelled the regime from most towns and villages in the Quneitra area closed to the Israeli border. And the rebels recently seized the central prison in Daraa, freed hundreds of prisoners, and cleared regime checkpoints in the city.

Perhaps the most strategically damaging offensive to the regime right now, however, is the Latakia offensive that has been mounted by the Islamic Front in the northwest of the country along the coastal strip in the mainly Alawite pro-regime province of Latakia. They have quickly seized the Kasab border crossing. They are fighting for control of Kasab town right now and for a series of key observatories and observation posts around the area. This is the same province that includes the Russian naval base of Tartus, which is now, to some extent, under threat. And we have seen some significant and very fierce fighting in just the last 24 hours, which has improved the rebels' position and actually brought them onto the Mediterranean coastline in control of a small town on the coast for the first time in the history of the war. And they have also killed President Assad's cousin, Hilal Assad, who was the head of the Syrian National Defense Forces.

So I think the issue is not that the regime is winning. The issue is that neither side is winning. They are both very much in the fight. They all believe that they can still win, provided they just ratchet up the violence enough. And what we need to do—and I fully agree with Assistant Secretary Patterson on this—is we need to change the facts on the ground. We need to change the military calculus of the regime by altering its belief that it can win militarily.

I am over time. So I will stop with my initial remarks, but I am very happy to talk in detail about all of those issues and also military options going forward.

[The prepared statement of Dr. Kilcullen follows:]

PREPARED STATEMENT OF DR. DAVID J. KILCULLEN

Mr Chairman (Senator Menendez), Ranking Member (Senator Corker), members of the committee, thank you for the opportunity to testify today on options for future U.S. policy on Syria. I'd like to offer an assessment of the conflict, and of actions the United States might take—alone or with allies—to improve the prospects for a peaceful and strategically acceptable solution. With your permission I plan to limit my initial remarks to three issues: an overview of the current situation in and around Syria; a discussion of realistic goals; and an outline of policy options.

CURRENT SITUATION: AN ESCALATING STALEMATE

The civil war in Syria entered its fourth year this month. Since March 2011, the conflict has escalated from initial mass uprisings by an unarmed, diverse collection of nationalist, pro-democracy and dissident groups, into a fragmented, complex, and increasingly violent sectarian insurgency against an entrenched regime.

The regime doesn't entirely control any major city except downtown Damascus. In every other major population center it has either been replaced by rebel governance structures, or rural guerrillas and urban resisters are contesting its control. The Syrian countryside, outlying districts, and smaller towns are heavily contested, and even in formally regime-controlled areas there are active resistance groups and asymmetric attacks against the government.

Even as the regime has lost control of roughly 75 percent of Syria's territory, rebel groups have fractured along sectarian, ideological, regional, or ethnic lines. This fragmentation has begun to reverse itself in recent months, with the emergence of the Islamic Front (composed of seven Islamist factions), the Southern Front comprising a loose alliance of almost 50 local groups in the south, and the reinvigoration of the Syrian Military Council with new leadership in recent weeks.

In general terms, the conflict is in what we might call an "escalating stalemate."

Neither the regime nor the rebels can achieve outright military victory, yet both sides still believe they can win, and are escalating violence to improve their position. This has resulted in spring offensives by both the regime and the rebels, a surge of violence against civilians, and increased flows of refugees and internally displaced persons. Neither side can win under present circumstances, but that doesn't mean the conflict is static or winding down—on the contrary, all sides are ratcheting up the violence.

The regime's Qalamoun offensive is focused on cementing control of a triangle of territory from Aleppo in the north, to Damascus, and west to the Lebanese border and the Mediterranean coast. Since January, government forces have captured the town of Yabroud near the Lebanese border, advanced west of Homs to seize three towns and clear a rebel stronghold in the Crusader castle of Krak des Chevaliers, and killed a large number of rebels in Ghouta, on the eastern edge of Damascus (where the regime used chemical weapons to kill up to 1,400 people in August 2013).

Over the past year the government has also consolidated and professionalized dozens of irregular groups (including the shabiha gangs active early in the fighting, and numerous local sectarian and militia groups), unifying them into the National Defense Forces, a force of 60,000 fighters which has become an important regime tool in holding ground, providing local security garrisons, and guarding supply lines and installations, freeing up the Syrian Arab Army for major combat operations.

But, in my view, recent media reports that "the regime is winning" significantly overstate the case. In the same timeframe as the government offensive, the rebels have mounted three successful major offensives of their own.

Just in the last month, insurgents seized districts on the outskirts of Aleppo City, while increasing their control in the wider Aleppo and Idlib provinces, allowing them to cut off regime outposts in the north. In the northeast, a separate rebel offensive has cleared regime positions in Deir ez Zor and along the Euphrates River, while in the south, the Southern Front has expelled the regime from most towns and villages in the Quneitra area near the Israeli border. The rebels seized the central prison in Daraa, freed hundreds of prisoners, and cleared regime checkpoints in the city.

Perhaps most strategically threatening to the regime, the Islamic Front, Jabhat al-Nusra and Ahrar al-Sham launched a joint offensive last week in the northwest, in the mainly Alawite pro-regime Latakia province. They quickly seized the Kasab border crossing and are fighting for control of Kasab town, potentially opening up a new rebel supply line from Turkey, threatening regime control of a key coastal province that includes the Russian naval base at Tartus, and (in fierce fighting this past Sunday) killing Hilal Assad, head of the Syrian National Defense Forces—the regime's paramilitary forces—who is also President Bashar al-Assad's cousin.

So, despite regime successes, and a surge of violence that has seen almost 2,500 civilians killed in barrel bombings of residential areas since last November, and has pushed total deaths in the conflict to more than 146,000, neither the regime nor the rebels have the upper hand, both are still in the fight, and the war is—if anything—ramping up into an increasingly bloody guerrilla conflict.

The inability of each side to prevail outright in military terms is reflected in the numbers, particularly the correlation of forces. Syrian regime forces of all kinds, including foreign allies, number between 190,000 and 341,000, while opposition forces (both Arab and Kurdish, and including foreign fighters) number between 135,000 and 211,000. Based on these ranges, the best-case force ratio for the regime is roughly 2.5 to 1, and the best case for the rebels is about 1.1. Given Syria's overall population size of 22 million, this leaves the government far short of the traditional 3:1 superiority for victory in a conventional conflict, and with only about half the ratio of 20 counterinsurgents per 1,000 population that is traditionally expected for success in a counterinsurgency campaign. The rebels have even less ability to prevail in a conventional conflict, though they are somewhat more likely to achieve success via a protracted insurgent strategy. Clearly, numbers are not everything and do not predict a particular outcome—in this case, however, they suggest that the regime's confidence in a military victory is sorely misplaced.

Further afield, the conflict is de-stabilizing Syria's neighbors. Lebanon, Turkey, and Jordan have been swamped by more than 4 million refugees, an influx that has created stresses on public health, water, public safety, electricity, and food and medical supplies. Syria is now the largest source of refugees on the planet, with 2.5 million refugees overseas, on top of another 6.5 million internally displaced persons. I should point out that 1.2 million of these refugees and IDPs are children, 425,000 of them under 5 years old, while boys as young as 12 have been forced to fight as child soldiers or deliberately targeted for torture and execution in order to punish and coerce their communities.

The water shortage created by the refugee crisis has made Jordan the third-most water-insecure country in the world, and has posed severe humanitarian challenges for Turkey and Lebanon. Lebanon has experienced internal conflict, as Hezbollah has sent 3,000–5,000 fighters to support the Assad regime, undermining its claim to put Lebanon first and to act as protector of Sunni as well as Shia communities. In Iraq, we've seen a reemergence of AQI, in part because of a spillover of conflict from Syria, and the movement of both pro-regime and pro-rebel fighters and supplies through Iraq into and out of Syria.

The fighting threatens to draw in Syria's neighbors more directly: Syrian aircraft have recently been shot down by Jordan, Lebanon, and Turkey; there's been an Israeli strike on Syrian territory near Quneitra, and Syria's relations with its neighbors (excluding Iraq) are at an all-time low.

At the same time, the regime's loss of control in Kurdish regions has contributed to the appearance of a de facto autonomous region of Syrian Kurdistan, centered on Hassakeh and linked both to the PKK in southern Turkey via the PYD, and to

Iraq's Kurdish Regional Government via the Kurdish National Council. We're seeing PYD begin to come out on top in an internal struggle for control in Kurdish regions of Syria, establishing its own local governance structures, and excluding the regime from large parts of the country. PYD's control is contested (both by other Kurdish groups and Islamist groups such as ISIL) but it's not beyond the bounds of possibility that one outcome of the Syrian conflict may be the emergence of an independent Kurdistan, which—while it might be welcomed both by Kurds and by some countries in the region—would fundamentally affect the geostrategic balance in this part of the middle east.

Inside Syria, the Islamic State of Iraq and the Levant (ISIL) has been pushed back by the Islamic Front and other rebel groups from its high-water mark of late 2013, so that it is now concentrated in Raqqa City in the northeast, where its support is steadily eroding due to its policy of beheadings, kidnappings, public torture, and the imposition of extremely strict Islamic codes. But the group still fields 6,000–7,000 fighters, many of them foreigners from Iraq and the wider region.

Further afield, we're seeing vast numbers of foreign fighters coming from as far away as Morocco, Tunisia, Libya, Egypt, the Gulf States, the Caucasus, Western Europe, and Southeast Asia. The scale of foreign fighter flows into Syria is now approximately 10 to 12 times the size of what we saw in Iraq, and involves fighters coming into the country to support both the regime and rebel groups. As Matthew Levitt recently testified before this committee, many of these fighters can eventually be expected to return to their home countries, with a significant regional destabilizing effect.

For its part, the regime is increasingly dependent on foreign fighters from Hezbollah, on advisers and technical support from Iran (including the Iranian Revolutionary Guards Corps and the Quds Force) and on technical support, financial assistance, logistics and maintenance from Russia—especially for its air force. Russia also continues to provide armored vehicles, precision munitions (in limited numbers) and remotely piloted aircraft to the regime. Iran provides subsidized fuel, ammunition, and weapons, and has sent military advisers to train the paramilitary National Defense Forces, collect intelligence, and assist in command and control. Hezbollah special troops have been advising and leading Syrian military units, and showed their familiarity with urban guerrilla operations during the regime's Qusayr offensive last summer.

One group of foreign fighters is especially worth noting—Chechens from the Caucasus, Uzbeks from Central Asia, and Tatars from the Crimea have traveled to Syria in recent years to fight a key Russian ally, learn military skills and participate in the jihad at a time when Russian operations, and those of Russia's local allies, have made it harder to operate in the Caucasus. The Chechen military commander Muhammad al-Shishani, killed earlier this year, commanded roughly 400 Chechen fighters of the Jaish al-Muhajirin wal Ansar (the Army of Emigrants and Supporters), a group owing allegiance to the Islamic Emirate of the Caucasus, which fights under Jabhat al-Nusra within the Islamic Front. Other well-known fighters include Omar al-Shishani, a commander within ISIL, and Abdul Karim Krymsky, a Crimean Tatar from Ukraine, who is deputy emir of the Army of Emigrants and Supporters. Given recent developments in Crimea, it's an open question as to whether these fighters may now see an opportunity to return to Russian-controlled territory in the Caucasus and Ukraine.

WHY SHOULD THE UNITED STATES CARE, AND WHAT CAN WE DO?

It's worth pausing to ask why any of this matters to the United States, why we ought to consider doing anything about it, and if so what we can do.

I think there are three main reasons why the situation in Syria matters to us:

First and most importantly, the conflict is a massive humanitarian tragedy, and one that is escalating—the violence is ratcheting up, and it can go up a lot further before the parties to the conflict accept the need for a negotiated settlement, if they ever do. Genocidal sectarian and ethnic rhetoric is coming from several rebel groups, backing Syria's large Alawite community into a corner and leaving them little current option but to support the regime, despite feelings of resentment and disillusionment against the government among many. The regime has killed thousands of innocent civilians with chemical weapons and barrel bombs, and through denial of basic services like food, water, and medical assistance to civilians in rebel-controlled areas. It has also tortured something like 11,000 detainees to death over the course of the conflict. Things could still get much, much worse, with enormous humanitarian impact, but also with the potential to create a longstanding, violent, ethnosectarian conflict across the whole region for decades to come.

Secondly, the conflict in Syria is destroying stability in Iraq. Syria is not the only cause of instability in Iraq, but the conflict has revived AQI, has contributed to a collapse in relations between the KRG and Baghdad, and has launched several new Sunni Arab rebel groups who are now holding territory in areas that were cleared of the insurgency back in 2007–2008. Violence in Iraq is now at levels not seen since the worst days of the war in 2006. There's a very real risk that a continued escalation in Syria could fatally undermine everything that we worked for: the relative stability and safety that 1.5 million Americans fought for in Iraq over the last decade (and for which 4,500 Americans died and 30,000 were wounded) rendering the whole massive Iraq effort for naught.

Finally, the conflict threatens key allies—Jordan, Turkey, Israel, Lebanon, and countries further afield are all experiencing the spillover of violence, refugee movement, and overstress that the war has created, and they could either be drawn into the conflict or have their stability and security significantly undermined by it. The conflict in Syria not only harms millions of innocents, but it also undermines our whole strategic position in the broader region.

I think these facts suggest that we should do something, but it's worth asking if there's anything that we can do, beyond what we are already doing. The national mood is clearly against another war, but the American people have often been offered a false choice between doing nothing, and committing ground combat forces to a full-scale invasion (''boots on the ground''). I don't believe such an all-or-nothing approach is helpful, and indeed there are several options short of major conflict that are worth considering. Before looking at policy options, however, we need to consider what our goals should be.

POLICY GOALS

Current U.S. policy goals, to the extent that they've been clearly articulated, seem to be to offer humanitarian assistance inside Syria; to contain regional conflict; and to disrupt foreign fighter flows further afield. Our actions to date have sought to ameliorate conditions on the ground, contain regional destabilization by reassuring partners and friends, and disrupt flows of foreign fighters, military material, illicit goods and finances into and out of the conflict.

U.S. policymakers have previously suggested that President Assad needs to step down, but with a fragmented and increasingly radicalized opposition our leaders have often seemed to shy away from that goal, for fear of what a successor regime might look like. And, perhaps sensing our ambivalence, in the Geneva talks the Syrian negotiators rejected even the notion of a transitional government: the regime instead is planning to hold national elections in June to cement President Assad in power for another term.

The United States also backed away from our own announced redline in September 2013, when we failed to follow through on previous threats to act against regime targets in the wake of the Ghouta chemical attack, and instead allowed the regime to negotiate for a gradual dismantling of its weapons stocks. To date only about 50 percent of Syrian chemical weapons have been transported to Latakia for destruction, the Syrian Government has missed several deadlines set by OPCW, and it is currently negotiating for a further extension of the handover deadline. The weapons destruction process is on hold because of the breakdown in cooperation between the United States and Russia after Russia's annexation of Crimea, and the regime seems in no hurry to complete the dismantling of its weapons, since once the weapons are no longer there, and the regime is no longer needed to safeguard them, the Syrian Government's leverage with the international community will be dramatically eroded. Meanwhile our own diplomatic leverage is negligible, in part because of our demonstrated lack of willingness to back diplomacy with action. In effect, in 2013, we called our own bluff, and our interlocutors—Iran, Russia, and the Syrian Government—are treating us accordingly.

FUTURE POLICY OPTIONS

I want to suggest that the goals that have animated U.S. policy to date, far from being overly ambitious, have actually been too minimalist. We've sought to contain and manage the conflict, but not to end it. Unsurprisingly, we've found it extraordinarily difficult to rally allies or the American people around such a minimal goal, which offers little positive result to offset its undeniable costs.

I would argue that our approach should instead be to seek an end to the conflict via a negotiated settlement, and to increasingly telegraph our willingness to use military means to force that outcome. Our use of force in this case would serve the strategic purpose of convincing the regime that it can't win militarily and needs to seek a peaceful solution. Our preference would be for indirect means where possible, but our policy would contemplate direct military action if needed. If the problem is that both sides still think they can win militarily, and thus don't feel that they need to negotiate, then the solution is to convince one or both sides that it cannot win and that its best option is to talk. Without that willingness to negotiate, founded on a realization that there's no chance of military victory, the conflict is likely to just keep ratcheting up, with all the negative consequences discussed already.

Some specific policy recommendations, then:

1. *Ignore the June elections.* We should ignore the regime's planned elections scheduled for this summer, which will certainly result in a manipulated landslide vote in President Assad's favor. The regime's strategy at present seems to be to use the Geneva II process to buy time, while it ramps up military operations in Syria to expand the territory and population it controls, using its military success to set the conditions for the Presidential elections, which are the key to President Assad's medium-term strategy to stay in office. We need to let it be known now that any election result achieved under these conditions would be illegitimate and invalid. And when the elections do inevitably take place, we should treat the result as null and void.

2. *Exploit linkages with other issues.* We should exploit linkages between Syria and other issues: particularly, Russia's intervention in the Ukraine and the increasing economic cost and political isolation that Moscow will experience as a result. With several hundred fighters from the Caucasus, including Crimean Tatars, operating in Syria, and the recent rebel offensive in Latakia threatening Russia's naval presence, there's a clear potential for violence in Syria to spread to Russian-controlled territory. Over time, establishing a linkage between Russia's actions in Ukraine and its support for the Assad regime may offer an opening to convince Russia to cease its active support and perhaps even to help convince the regime that a negotiated solution is in all parties' best interest.

3. *Focus on peace-building at the local level.* As we think about what a negotiated solution might look like, one key element is to build local momentum toward a peaceful settlement of the conflict. A striking aspect of the Geneva II talks (mentioned in the attached research paper prepared by our Syria field research team) was how few Syrians saw either the regime, or the representatives negotiating in Geneva on behalf of the rebels, as legitimate representatives of the Syrian people. In a series of surveys conducted in Aleppo—Syria's largest city and one of the most heavily affected by conflict—the most common response to question "Who is the legitimate representative of the Syrian people?" was "No one." The combined total of support for both the rebel negotiators and the regime across all surveys conducted was never higher than 12 percent, suggesting that almost 9 out of 10 Syrians had no faith in (and therefore very low expectations of) the Geneva process. If subsequent peace talks are to succeed, Syrians at the local level must develop cross-community interest in a peaceful settlement.

4. *Expand assistance programs to the opposition.* Ultimately, however, if a peace process is to have any chance, it must begin from a different set of facts on the ground than currently exist and, in particular, the Syrian regime must realize that it has no chance of a military victory. To underline this point, the international community—including the United States—should continue and, if possible, expand assistance to the opposition, across four dimensions: humanitarian assistance; non-lethal technical support; training and advisory support; and lethal technical weapons systems:

- Humanitarian assistance (including food, water, medical support, and education) is key to defeating the regime's strategy of denying essential humanitarian supplies and services to opposition areas. We can therefore expect continued regime opposition to the distribution of humanitarian assistance, but this provides an opportunity not only to assist Syria's civilian population but also to break the regime's stranglehold on besieged areas.

- Nonlethal technical support to rebel forces, including communications equipment, medical supplies, clothing and equipment, vehicles and logistics has been a key motivator for rebel groups to join together into more cohesive organizations such as the Southern Front. For most of the conflict, a unifying factor among regime supporters has been the centralization of funding and assistance through the Syrian Government, which has tended to draw groups together. As the formation of the Southern Front shows, it's possible for international assistance to the opposition to have a similar unifying effect. As new rebel offensives along Syria's borders open up more access points, we should expand this assistance—in geographical spread, in volume, and in quality.

- Training and advisory support, whether delivered directly by U.S. personnel or by allies or civilian contractors, has the potential to raise the fighting quality of rebel forces. This is important not only because it helps them combat the regime more effectively, but because one of the key aspects in the attractiveness of extremist jihadi groups is their reputation for greater military competence, skills, and effectiveness in the field. To the extent that we can help improve the command and planning skills, tactical quality and operational effectiveness of nonjihadist rebel groups in Syria, we can not only help redress the unfavorable correlation of forces vis-a-vis the regime, but can also strengthen secular, nationalist, pro-civil society groups in relation to more extreme factions of the insurgency.

- Lethal technical weapons support—including small arms and light weapons, heavier artillery/mortars and their associated technical fire control systems, and (most importantly) advanced man-portable and vehicle-mounted air defense systems capable of defeating regime air platforms and helicopter-launched ''barrel bomb'' attacks on civilians, would make a critical difference in the conflict. As experience in Afghanistan, Libya, Iraq and elsewhere has shown, with appropriate safeguards and oversight, and with careful selection of weapon types and management of ammunition availability, the threat of terrorist acquisition of such weapons is relatively manageable.

5. *Plan for limited military strikes.* No option—including military options—should be off the table at this point. The policy options I have suggested here work best when they work together, where the threat of force increases the leverage of our diplomats while diplomatic efforts toward a peaceful settlement help improve the chances of a successful military action. We should initiate planning toward a campaign—focusing on limited air strikes supported by airborne and ground tactical effects controllers, with limited special operations forces advisory support, intelligence support and naval operations offshore—designed to simultaneously guarantee the protection of at-risk civilians via safe zones, no-fly areas and humanitarian corridors, and to target critical regime capabilities in order to convince the regime that its best option is to negotiate an end to the conflict, most likely via a transitional coalition government under international supervision. Extremist groups undermining such a peaceful outcome would become legitimate targets in a subsequent phase of such a campaign. We may, for example, publish a list of regime targets and capabilities, several of which may be struck in retaliation for attacks on civilians, while simultaneously opening up humanitarian corridors or safe zones and denying the regime the ability to move armored units, mount air strikes or receive resupply via sea and air from its allies.

This would entail planning for the possibility of a coalition military campaign on roughly the scale of the Kosovo or Libya interventions, and would undoubtedly not be without human and financial cost, but it would have the advantage of promoting a clear and achievable political goal, after repeated attempts at negotiations and other peaceful means had failed, and would avoid the scenario of regime collapse and the emergence of a jihadi state in Syria.

I want to emphasize in closing that I'm not suggesting we immediately jump to a military option, nor that such an option would be cost-free or guaranteed to work. My point is merely that we do have a range of options short of a major ground operation, that we need to demonstrate a willingness to consider military action if we are to restore some leverage to our diplomatic efforts in the wake of last year's loss of credibility, and that (given the increasing international isolation and economic strain experienced by Syria's major ally, Russia) this may be an opportunity to push for a peaceful, negotiated outcome to the conflict, rather than the present escalating stalemate. Ultimately, we should continue to seek a peaceful solution through diplomacy, but paradoxically the effectiveness of our diplomatic initiatives (and hence the prospects for peace) may depend on our willingness to plan for, and ultimately use, a measure of military force.

[EDITOR'S NOTE.—The research paper mentioned above was too voluminous to include in the printed hearing. It will be retained in the permanent record of the committee.]

The CHAIRMAN. We will look forward in the Q&A to picking up on your last statement, which is how does one change those calculations.

Dr. Nasr.

STATEMENT OF DR. VALI NASR, DEAN, JOHNS HOPKINS SCHOOL OF ADVANCED INTERNATIONAL STUDIES, WASHINGTON, DC

Dr. NASR. Good afternoon. Thank you, Mr. Chairman, Ranking Member Corker, and members of the committee, for giving me this opportunity to testify before you about this very important issue.

I will limit my testimony to a discussion of our diplomatic strategy.

Since 2011, the crisis in Syria has evolved from an uprising of the people in a quest for freedom into a civil war which has now broad international and regional implications. I agree with Dr. Kilcullen that there is no immediate sign of an end to the fighting, that neither the Assad regime nor the opposition is currently strong enough to win, and the civil war is bound to continue moving toward what looks like an intractable stalemate.

I think this poses some serious national security challenges to the United States and a threat to global security, first, because I think the humanitarian crisis has evolved into a regional security issue; secondly, the proliferation and entrenchment of extremism is now a major concern; and thirdly, because the Syria conflict has evolved into a regional struggle for power on the one side between Turkey, Qatar, and Saudi Arabia and, much more importantly, between Iran and Saudi Arabia.

Now, the international effort led by the United Nations in two rounds of talks in Geneva have failed to end the war. I think those efforts were primarily focused on reaching an agreement between the United States and Russia, which actually has strategic, economic, and historical motivations to support the Assad regime in power.

The United States went to Geneva II believing that Assad's removal from power is essential to ending the conflict, whereas Russia's position is based on the fact that Syria is a case of a global threat by Islamic terrorism and extremism and that is the primary issue to be discussed.

However, it is important to note that the United States and Russia are not the main outside actors in Syria. Rather, both the Assad regime and the opposition are armed, financed, and supported by regional actors. The Assad regime owes its survival not to Russia but to Iran and its regional allies, Hezbollah and Iraqi militias whose military and intelligence support has kept the Assad regime from crumbling and then taking the offensive. Similarly, it is Turkey, Qatar, Kuwait, and Saudi Arabia that have financed and armed the opposition fighters, keeping up the pressure on Damascus.

I do not see any evidence of a United States military strategy. So as a result, all the focus is on a diplomatic strategy. I think repeating Geneva II will not achieve the intended result of ending the stalemate in Syria. First of all, United States-Russia dynamics have become more complicated by the Ukraine crisis. If these two nations could not agree on Syria before, it will be much more difficult to do so following the Russian annexation of Crimea.

Now, treating Russia as a partner from this point forward will actually cause resentment and cynicism in the Middle East. It will actually show that the United States is determined not to act in

Syria, even at the cost of aligning itself with Russia, despite what has happened in Ukraine, and it will also will give Russia an added opportunity to use Syria as a way of managing the Ukraine crisis.

Secondly, even if there was a United States-Russia agreement on Syria, it could not be implemented without the support of regional actors which have a stake in the conflict.

So I think there is need for a new approach to the diplomatic resolution of the Syria crisis, I think one that starts with the following assumption.

One is that regional actors now have far more at stake in this conflict than the United States or Russia.

The Syrian civil war is now integral to a regional struggle for power, the outcome of which will decide the balance of power between Saudi Arabia, Turkey, and Qatar on the one side, as I mentioned, Saudi Arabia and Iran. These regional powers are acting with the understanding that the future of the Middle East is being decided in Syria.

The Middle East, in the meantime, lacks any regional mechanisms that would allow these regional actors to resolve the conflict through any form of negotiations.

As a result, given these assumptions, the time has come for the United States and the international community to consider an approach that would actually take into account the interests and stakes of the regional actors.

Now, the Syrian conflict is happening at a time of big change in the region. We are seeing a collapse and inclusion of Egypt, traditionally the most important and influential Arab country. We are seeing and intensification of conflict between Qatar and Saudi Arabia. We are seeing a chilling of relations between Turkey and Saudi Arabia, and we are seeing an escalation of regional rivalry between Iran and Saudi Arabia.

Now, a diplomatic solution, nevertheless, would require the acquiescence and support of these powers, and therefore, the task I think before the international community as a first step is to bring an alignment between the positions of Qatar, Turkey, and Saudi Arabia, three American allies in the region that have enormous influence on both the political opposition and fighters on the ground but actually lack coordination, and their policies are not aligned together. Creating an alignment between these powers will actually help unify the Syrian opposition, which was one of the reasons why the Geneva talks was not taken seriously by Iran, Russia, and the Assad government and actually, in and of itself, is a changing of the facts on the ground short of military intervention.

I think it is much more important in the short run that the United Nations and the United States focus on shuttle diplomacy in the Middle East rather than convening a large-scale Geneva-like conference.

I will conclude my remarks at this point.

[The prepared statement of Dr. Nasr follows:]

Prepared Statement by Dr. Vali R. Nasr

Introduction

Thank you Mr. Chairman, Ranking Member Corker, members of the committee for this opportunity to testify before you on options for addressing the crisis in Syria after the Geneva II talks, and in particular on the geopolitical implications of the conflict.

My name is Vali Nasr and I am the Dean of the Paul H. Nitze School of Advanced International Studies at the Johns Hopkins University.

Since 2011, the crisis in Syria has evolved from an uprising of the people in a quest for freedom into a civil war with broad international and regional implications. There is no sign of an end to the fighting. Neither the Assad regime nor the opposition is strong enough to win, and the civil war is bound to continue, moving toward an intractable stalemate.

The international effort led by the United Nations in two rounds of talks in Geneva failed to end the war. Those efforts focused primarily on bringing about an agreement between the United States and Russia, which has strategic, economic, and historical motivations to support the Assad regime. That goal proved elusive because

—The United Nations failed to bridge the gap between the United States and Russia. The United States sees Assad's removal from power as essential to ending the conflict, and therefore saw Geneva talks as the mechanism for replacing the Assad regime with a transitional government. Russia sees the problem in Syria as one of extremism and Islamic terrorism. Furthermore, Russia does not envision an outcome in which Assad steps down; in the unlikely event that Assad ever did step down, Russia does not believe it would lead to a viable government that can rule Syria.

—The Geneva talks downplayed the importance of regional actors. The United States and Russia are critical to galvanizing the international community around a solution to the Syrian crisis. Cooperation between the two is important in the United Nations Security Council, as was evident in securing an agreement to dismantle Syria's stockpile of chemical weapons.

However, the United States and Russia are not the main outside actors in Syria. Rather, both the Assad regime and the opposition are armed, financed, and supported by regional actors. The Assad regime owes its survival not to Russia but to Iran and its regional allies, Lebanon's Hezbollah and Iraq's Shia militias whose military and intelligence support has kept Assad's forces from crumbling and then taking the offensive. Similarly, it is Turkey, Qatar, Kuwait, and Saudi Arabia that have financed and armed the rebels, keeping up the opposition's pressure on Damascus.

Repeating Geneva II will not achieve the intended result of ending the stalemate in Syria. First, U.S.-Russia dynamics have become more complicated by the crisis in Ukraine. If the two nations could not agree on Syria before, it will be all the more difficult to do so following the Russian annexation of Crimea. Second, even if there was a U.S.-Russian agreement on Syria, it could not be implemented without the support of regional actors with stakes in the conflict.

There is need for a new approach to Syria, one that starts with the following assumptions:

—The regional actors have far more at stake in this conflict than the United States or Russia.

—The Syrian civil war is integral to the regional struggle for power. Its outcome will decide the balance of power between Saudi Arabia and Turkey, Saudi Arabia and Qatar, and most significantly, Saudi Arabia and Iran. These regional powers are acting with the understanding that the future of the Middle East will be decided in Syria.

—The civil war has touched off regionwide sectarian tensions that have polarized opinion on Syria and cast the conflict as a zero-sum struggle for power between Shias and Sunnis.

—The Syrian refugee crisis has become a regional security challenge. The number of refugees in Lebanon, Jordan, Iraq, and Turkey is an economic burden and political threat to those countries—and this problem will only grow as more refugees escape the fighting.

—The Middle East lacks any regional mechanisms that would allow regional actors to resolve this conflict.

Given these assumptions, the time has come for the United States and the international community to consider a new diplomatic approach that incorporates the interests and stakes of all regional powers heavily invested in Syria.

THE REGIONAL ACTORS' STAKE IN SYRIA

The Syrian conflict is happening at a time of geostrategic change, domestic turmoil, and rebalancing of power in the Middle East. Egypt, the largest and traditionally most influential Arab country, is preoccupied with internal problems. Meanwhile, Qatar, Turkey, Saudi Arabia and Iran have all amplified their engagement in Syria to tilt the balance of power in favor of their particular geopolitical interests.

Qatar

Qatar has intensified its regional role, and that has been an irritant to its old rival, Saudi Arabia. Qatar sees its role in Syria as part of its broader design to influence regional trends, which also includes deep engagement in Libya and Egypt. Qatar's support in Syria has been important to key elements of the political opposition and fighters on the ground.

Turkey

Turkey shares a long border with Syria and is now home to a large Syrian refugee population. Turkey's policy toward Syria was premised on the assumption that the Assad regime would fall quickly. Three years on, this assumption is no longer self-evident, and Turkey finds itself threatened by chaos and growing extremism next door. Turkey is worried that Syria's sectarian tensions would spill over into Turkey, and also that the impact of the fighting on Syrian Kurds would impact Turkey's own delicate Kurdish situation.

Turkey no longer has influence with the government in Damascus, and it has had to compete with Saudi Arabia and Qatar for influence over the opposition. In addition, preoccupation with domestic issues has limited Turkey's ability to exercise control over developments in Syria. These circumstances are pushing Turkey to look for a strategy to end the Syrian civil war.

Saudi Arabia

Saudi Arabia has been unhappy with Turkey's growing influence in the Middle East. Saudi Arabia, Qatar, and Turkey have been competing for influence over the Syrian opposition—which explains in part the opposition's inability to put up a united front before the Assad regime.

More important, Saudi Arabia sees the outcome in Syria as critical to checking and even reversing Iran's regional influence. If the Assad regime falls, Iran would suffer a strategic blow that could also weaken its position in Lebanon and Iraq.

Iran

Iran by the same token sees the survival of Assad's regime as a vital strategic imperative. The appearance of defeat in Syria would weaken Iran's regional influence, but also make it more difficult for Iran to continue negotiations with P5+1—for fear that its perceived weakness would make the international six-party team unyielding.

RECOMMENDATIONS

The time when the Syria conflict could have ended with an agreement between the United States and Russia has passed.

Currently the four Middle East powers—Qatar, Turkey, Saudi Arabia, and Iran—have far higher stakes in Syria than the United States and Russia, hence their heavy investments in deciding the outcome. A diplomatic solution must have their acquiescence and support.

The task remains before all of us to facilitate an agreement to end this war. The United States and the international community could provide the necessary link to get the regional backers of the warring factions to start a diplomatic process. In particular, the United States has strong ties with Qatar, Turkey, and Saudi Arabia and should use that influence to bring their positions in Syria into alignment.

As a first step, the United States and its European allies should focus diplomatic attention on

—Bringing Saudi, Qatari and Turkish positions on Syria into alignment;

—Unifying the Syrian opposition;

—Laying the groundwork for a regional diplomatic framework for ending the war in Syria. That framework could set the parameters for Iran and Iraq's participation in the process.

The CHAIRMAN. Mr. Egeland.

STATEMENT OF JAN EGELAND, SECRETARY GENERAL, NORWEGIAN REFUGEE COUNCIL, OSLO, NORWAY

Mr. EGELAND. Thank you very much, Chairman Menendez, Ranking Member Corker, members of the committee.

I am the Secretary General of the Norwegian Refugee Council. We have 1,000 staff members on the ground in and around Syria. We assist 700,000 Syrian displaced and refugees.

Through 30 years of humanitarian work, I have visited most of the major war zones and disaster zones of the past generation. I have never, ever before witnessed the kind of suffering that we now see in Syria.

Last month, when I visited Syria and Lebanon this time—it was my sixth visit to the region since the war started—I met Myriam, this 8-year-old girl, who told me that her home was destroyed by rockets 1 year ago. Then her family joined the 6.5 million internally displaced in Syria. Twice more, their improvised homes were destroyed by the fighting, and in the end, they ended up—the family—among the 1 million refugees in Lebanon. Myriam has one big dream, and that is to become a medical doctor because she wants to return to her country and treat the injured and the ill.

I would like now, since I did a detailed written testimony, only to make four following points in answering to the questions I got in the e-mail beforehand.

First, we need the United States to pursue political dialogue with all sides and push for respect of the laws of war and for conflict resolution talks. With Russia, the United States brought about an agreement to destroy the chemical weapons. We have not had any commensurate humanitarian agreement or humanitarian cease-fire reached. It should not be more easy to reach and retrieve chemical weapons than it is to reach and help evacuate women and children from besieged cities. As humanitarians, we see the horrible effects of political paralysis every day. We ask that all countries with leverage on the parties, on their sponsors, or on their suppliers must put pressure where they can.

Second point. The U.S. policy needs to work for unimpeded aid delivery to all civilians caught in the cross-fire or caught in the many besieged towns. Millions with unmet needs can most directly be reached from across Syria's borders. The time has come, in our view, for the U.S. Government, other donors, the United Nations, and neighboring countries to put their full weight behind full-scale and effective cross-border relief. And the U.N. Security Council Resolution 2139 and international law give a clear legal basis for such cross-border relief.

My third point. The U.S. policy must ensure that all humanitarian assistance to Syria is, and is perceived to be, impartial, neutral, and independent from political agendas. I repeat. The humanitarian relief needs to be impartial and neutral and independent from political agendas. It is dangerous for the civilians we help and for our fieldworkers on the ground if humanitarian relief is politicized or militarized. So, for example, counterterror laws must not be applied in this case in a way that harms our ability to provide impartial relief to women and children in disputed areas.

Finally, the United States is, indeed, the world's greatest donor and we thank you for that. But increased funding is needed with the dramatic increase in refugees, displaced, and war-affected. Only 12.5 percent of the overall U.N.-led appeals for the region and for Syria of $6.5 billion has been met for 2014—12.5 percent so far. Syria's neighbors have so far generously accepted 2.5 million refugees and more come every single day. The region faces instability and social and economic collapse. Increased aid is urgently needed in particular to Lebanon and Jordan. And the United States, European countries like my own must allow more Syrian refugees to cross their borders.

So, Mr. Chairman, we need to provide hope to the 6 million affected Syrian children. If they lose all hope, we will not only end up with unspeakable misery, but with a more unstable Middle East and a world community that is unstable. It is, therefore, in keeping with our values and in our interests to do more to help a future for the children of Syria.

Thank you.

[The prepared statement of Mr. Egeland follows:]

PREPARED STATEMENT OF JAN EGELAND

INTRODUCTION

Chairman Menendez, Ranking Member Corker, and members of the committee, I thank you for this opportunity to input into your deliberations on the next steps for U.S. Policy. Let me also applaud the efforts you have made to bring attention to the plight of millions of Syrians, who continue to suffer as a result of this appalling conflict, now entering its 4th year.

I am the Secretary General of the Norwegian Refugee Council (NRC), an independent, humanitarian nongovernment organization that assists and protects millions of displaced people worldwide, including more than 700,000 Syrians across the Middle East.

I have been active in humanitarian and human rights work for more than 30 years and have visited many of the worst war- and disaster-zones of this past generation. I have never before seen the scale of suffering now present in Syria. Syrian families, and in particular the Syrian youth, are losing hope fast. We must restore hope, rebuild schools and provide a future for Syria's children.

I have previously had the opportunity to come to Congress to discuss the humanitarian challenges we have faced elsewhere in the world. I have seen how bipartisan support in and from this Senate has helped mobilize relief and hope for societies plagued by war and repression—from Darfur to northern Uganda and eastern Congo. Your support can help us again as we face even greater challenges in Syria.

Last month I was back in Syria and Lebanon—my sixth visit to this region since the war broke out. I saw once more the extreme challenges faced by the U.N., NGOs, and the Red Cross/Crescent in accessing the millions of people denied food, water, and medical supplies across the country. While I was there, extremely challenging negotiations to evacuate civilians from the besieged Old City of Homs were taking place. Painstaking efforts to agree a local cease-fire with a multitude of warring parties did not prevent U.N. and Red Crescent colleagues being shot at while entering Homs.

With the heroic efforts of Syrian and expatriate humanitarian workers operating across the country, assistance is reaching many parts of Syria and lives are being saved. However, it is nowhere near enough. Too many defenseless and suffering civilians are not being reached and the risks that humanitarians are forced to take in their daily work are totally unacceptable.

And the situation is not getting better. A year ago I traveled to the city of Aleppo and witnessed how desperate mothers, fathers, and neighbors were searching with their hands through the rubble of their destroyed apartment, trying desperately to find their own children, relatives, or friends. Missiles had hit heavily populated civilian areas the night before. After seeing the scale of suffering, I could not believe that the conflict could get any worse—but it has. Twice as many people in Syria are now dead or in urgent need of aid as when I was in Aleppo.

The stories I hear from Syrians who have fled the violence and from aid-workers are horrific: With active conflict, widespread disregard for basic moral and ethical standards, as well as the excessive restrictions imposed by the Syrian Government and opposition forces on humanitarian operations, millions of Syrians continue to be denied access to lifesaving humanitarian aid. The bureaucratic hurdles of some neighboring countries are further complicating our ability to operate. We request your further support to compel the Government of Syria and warring parties to remove all barriers to our operations so that millions of people can access the aid they urgently need and are entitled to. With your assistance, NRC and other dedicated aid agencies stand ready to cross battle lines, cross borders, cross rivers and mountains—whatever is required so that we can end the human suffering in Syria.

The crisis has seriously impacted Syria's regional neighbors, now hosting more than 2.5 million men, women, and children who have fled their homes. This equates to a population four times that of the District of Columbia. I have visited Lebanon and Jordan regularly over the last 2 years. Each time humanitarians, the people and authorities tell me that they have reached a breaking point. Yet, the flow of refugees keeps coming. I have spent time in Zaatari refugee camp in Jordan, which is one of the world's largest. No Syrian would choose to live there. But they have nowhere else to go. They have lost their homes, their jobs, and their loved ones. They have often suffered atrocities and unspeakable violence. A generation of Syrian children is growing up about to lose hope—and we risk losing them to poverty and despair.

Refugees in Zaatari and the millions more spread across the region need your help. As do the governments and communities who continue to demonstrate extraordinary generosity by hosting them. Lebanon is particularly in need of more direct financial and infrastructure support, and the U.S. can play an important part. By the end of next week, Lebanon will be hosting 1 million refugees, 230 refugees for every 1,000 Lebanese—the highest number of any country in recent history. Proportionally this equals 80 million refugees crossing the U.S. border in 18 months.

I want to take this opportunity to thank members of this committee, particularly the bipartisan leadership of Senators Kaine (D–VA) and Rubio (R–FL) for introducing Senate Resolution 384, which calls for the immediate and full implementation of U.N. Security Council 2139, including unimpeded humanitarian access, both across conflict lines and borders.

In this testimony, I will make four points to inform future U.S. policy:

- The U.S. should continue to pursue political dialogue with all sides in order to ensure respect for the Laws of War and ultimately resolve this senseless conflict. With Russia, the U.S. brought about an agreement to destroy Syria's chemical weapon stockpiles. We require this same leadership to uphold the humanitarian imperative and alleviate the suffering of the Syrian population, including the 9 million displaced. All countries with leverage over the parties to the conflict must put pressure where they can in order to seek a resolution to the crisis and respect for the Laws of War.

- U.S. policy needs to prioritize measures that ensure unimpeded aid delivery inside Syria. Syrians urgently need to be able to access more and better assistance and protection in or close to their homes. Government, donors and countries neighboring Syria must urgently facilitate the delivery of humanitarian assistance, across front-lines and across borders. As recognized by UNSC Resolution (S/RES/2139), International Humanitarian Law provides an unequivocal legal basis for undertaking cross-border operations, to all areas within Syria.

- U.S. policy should ensure that all humanitarian assistance to Syria is, and is perceived as impartial, neutral and independent from political agendas. Among related concerns, counterterrorism laws must not impact negatively on humanitarians' ability to maintain independence and ensure impartial provision of aid.

- The U.S., along with the international community, has a responsibility to help address the enormous challenges faced by Syria's neighbors. By generously accepting 2.5 million refugees, the region is facing the prospect of regional instability, and social and economic collapse. Increased humanitarian and development assistance is urgently needed. Furthermore, the U.S., Europe and other countries must share the responsibility and allow more refugees across their borders.

1. The U.S. should continue to pursue political dialogue

Our relief workers see each day the impact of the political stalemate on Syria. Syria is the worst humanitarian crisis in the 21st century. We all know the figures—more than 9 million people displaced, well over 100,000 killed, more than 5.5 million children at risk. During the 2 hours of this Senate hearing alone, 120 families will have been forced from their homes. These numbers are unfathomable when we consider that each individual represents immense human tragedy. Yet, the collective response of the international community remains woefully inadequate. A solution that ends this crisis must be your unequivocal priority.

As your former colleague in this committee, U.S. Secretary of State Kerry and other world leaders have repeatedly made clear; "There is no military solution to Syria, there is only a political solution and that will require leadership to bring people to the negotiating table."

Yet Geneva II generated no tangible results: No political solution, no lasting cease-fire, no end to the bloodshed and no alleviation of the unbearable suffering of the Syrian people. In spite of the enormous efforts of Special Envoy Brahimi, no concrete results were achieved. The millions of people who have been driven from their homes have had their hopes betrayed. We see shocking echoes of the horrors of Bosnia and Rwanda—and therefore a moral obligation to prevent a return to those dark days.

Only 6 month ago, the U.S., alongside Russia, led peaceful efforts to agree to a process to destroy Syria's weapons of mass destruction. Political progress is therefore possible—if there is enough political will. I call on the U.S. to resume this leadership role, for the Syrian people to realize their dream of a peaceful life. Syrians must be protected from all forms of violence, including the use of conventional weapons and barbaric "barrel bombs," which are responsible for the vast majority of the killings. To this end, I urge you to work with Russia and other members of the international community, and to use your influence with the warring parties and their allies, to ensure respect for international law and put an end to the conflict once and for all.

As urgent as political progress is, the millions of Syrians denied humanitarian aid cannot wait for negotiations to bear fruit. The humanitarian imperative to meet the immense needs and alleviate the suffering of ordinary Syrians cannot be a pawn traded within negotiations, or held hostage to political posturing. I urge you to do your uttermost to support the humanitarian endeavor in Syria, irrespective of political progress. There will be no winners at the end of this war, and whatever political end goals the international community has, the protection of civilians and respect for international humanitarian law cannot be compromised.

It is the persistent denial of humanitarian aid that I will now move on to address.

2. U.S. policy needs to prioritize measures to ensure unimpeded aid delivery

I have seen for myself how the Syrian Government and opposition forces impede the delivery of life-saving assistance on a daily basis, and how countries neighboring Syria place unreasonable administrative constraints on reputable NGOs. These practices have to end immediately.

I appeal for your help to ensure all parties to the conflict, particularly the Government of Syria, actively facilitate the delivery of life-saving assistance and protection. To be effective, this has to include ensuring humanitarian access from across Syria's borders—which is so often the most efficient route.

2.1 Impediments and denial of humanitarian access

There are countless examples of the deliberate and shameful denial of humanitarian assistance and protection. A few examples to illustrate:

- Aleppo governorate in northern Syria continues to experience air raids by the Syrian air force and clashes between military and armed opposition groups, as well as among the opposition groups, forcing more than 750,000 people to flee. The Government of Syria and some armed groups actively harass and sometimes even appear to target aid convoys. They stop humanitarian agencies at checkpoints, demand money and threaten aid workers with violence and illegal detention. They also attempt to divert humanitarian goods. The close proximity between southern Turkey and northern Aleppo means that assistance can and is being delivered from across the Syrian border, but delays and blockages at both sides of the crossings mean enough aid is not getting through.
- Many parts of Damascus and the surrounding rural areas have been entirely cut off from humanitarian assistance for up to a year due to the abhorrent use of siege tactics by government and some armed opposition forces and because of the ongoing active conflict. The barriers put in place by the Syrian Government, including restrictions on working with national NGOs, the refusal to let aid convoys travel and the ban on allowing agencies operating from Damascus to also deliver aid across borders, seriously inhibit the ability of aid agencies to realize the rights of those in need. Even areas located only a couple of miles from where aid agencies are based cannot be reached.
- Dar'a and Quneitra governorates in southern Syria have seen fierce fighting between Government and armed opposition groups. Shelling and aerial bom-

bardments continue to intensify throughout both governorates, leaving more than 245,000 people without access to even basic humanitarian assistance. Aid operations into southern Syria are considered dangerous due to the ongoing fighting. However, they would be possible if the Syrian Government gave permission for aid convoys to travel from Damascus or if cross-border aid routes could be utilized more effectively.

2.2 Besieged communities

Beyond these examples, an estimated 240,000 peoplex continue to be trapped in besieged communities, some for more than 1 year.

The use of medieval siege tactics and the deliberate starvation of hundreds of thousands of people have come to epitomize the brutality of the conflict. The recent evacuation of many civilians from the besieged areas of Homs has rightly received significant attention. More than 4,000 people faced deliberate starvation and had been trapped, without even basic supplies, for more than 600 days. While the media attention has died away, this crisis is not yet over. Fighting and shelling is ongoing and approximately 2,000 people remain in the Old City.

But, of Syria's many besieged civilians, 99 percent are not in Homs.

- In Nabul and Zahraa villages outside of Aleppo, an estimated 45,000 people continue to be effectively imprisoned, without food or drinking water. Despite multiple attempts at cease-fires, mediation has failed and these locations remain besieged by armed opposition groups and foreign fighters.
- In the Yarmouk refugee camp in Damascus, some 18,000 mainly Palestinian refugees remain under siege.
- In rural areas outside Damascus, an estimated 160,000 people are besieged. With the exception of some polio vaccines delivered by Syrian Arab Red Crescent, no aid has entered these areas since the siege began over 1 year ago.

These are just some of the gross violations of the Laws of War that continue unabated across Syria.

I appeal to you today to use your influence with all parties to prevent the continuation of these practices. Besieged populations must be set free and attacks on civilians, schools, and hospitals must stop. Cease-fires need to be supported and strengthened so that people can access assistance and humanitarian workers can operate. And governments' restrictions on humanitarian access, including from across borders, must end to enable those who need assistance to access it.

It is this last point that I would want to underline below, as an indispensable part of a future U.S. policy on Syria:

2.3 Improving humanitarian access

If we are to end to the humanitarian freefall in Syria the numerous constraints on access imposed by the Syrian authorities and armed groups must be reversed immediately. The intermittent refusal by neighboring governments to facilitate humanitarian access by reputable NGOs through the most efficient routes is also unacceptable. We urgently need the U.S. Government to use its influence with governments to ensure cross-border operations are better coordinated, funded, and implemented so that these vital operations can be expanded to assist the millions of people currently not receiving aid.

Millions of people who live in areas that are currently in need of aid can most directly be reached from across Syria's borders. To give one example, when I traveled by car to Aleppo from Turkey 1 year ago, it took me just over an hour to reach the city. It now can take days for U.N. convoys to reach Aleppo from Damascus, passing multiple checkpoints. The time has therefore come for the U.S. Government, international donors and countries neighboring Syria to urgently put their full weight behind the delivery of cross-border humanitarian assistance. The UNSC Resolution (S/RES/2139) and International Humanitarian Law provide the firm legal framework for implementing these operations. Humanitarian assistance is not a right that may be arbitrarily denied to Syrians in need, by their own government. The onus should therefore be on the Syrian Government to justify its rejection of cross-border humanitarian operations, including to opposition controlled areas, rather than on the need for the U.N. to obtain its permission.

I welcome the recent decision by the Syrian Government to allow the U.N. to restock aid supplies using the Nusaybin crossing from Turkey into north eastern Syria. This has the potential to allow tens of thousands of people (living in areas under the government's influence) to access aid. However, it falls far short of what is needed. The Nusaybin crossing is just one of many that need to be fully opened. The Syrian authorities must also allow humanitarian assistance to reach millions of civilians living in locations controlled by opposition forces. The use of the

Nusaybin border crossing by aid convoys is positive, but it can hardly be viewed as substantial progress toward the implementation of UNSC Resolution 2139.

There is no excuse for not facilitating a lot more cross-border aid operations. The registration processes for reputable aid agencies must be streamlined, existing border crossings must remain permanently open and new crossing points should be established for aid convoys. Setting up low-cost, fast-tracked system for granting residency and work permits for humanitarian staff in Turkey and other neighboring countries would greatly facilitate aid delivery.

Providing assistance from neighboring countries does not absolve the Syrian Government of its legal and moral responsibilities to ensure that aid delivered inside Syria, across battle lines, reaches all parts of the country. Having been to Damascus recently, I can tell you that humanitarian agencies are unable to operate freely from the capital. Delays with NGO registration, impediments to working with local aid agencies and severe travel restrictions are unacceptable and must be addressed urgently.

3. U.S. policy should ensure that all humanitarian assistance to Syria is, and is perceived as impartial, neutral, and independent from political agendas

Irrespective of how aid is delivered—whether from neighboring countries or from Damascus—access must be granted based on the humanitarian needs of the Syrian population, without political interference. The U.S. and other governments should ensure that humanitarian aid is easily identified as separate from other forms of nonhumanitarian supplies entering Syria.

Aid agencies in Syria face severe challenges with perception. Armed actors are suspicious and the population is increasingly impatient after 3 years of suffering. It is crucial that the U.S. Government ensures that its funding is provided in a manner that both is, and is perceived to be, impartial. The use of humanitarian aid by actors to gain influence, control, or buy the loyalty of civilian populations in order to further political goals cannot be tolerated. And aid which seeks to portray humanitarians or link humanitarians to any side of the conflict or to a political agenda is dangerous.

Respecting humanitarian principles also requires an honest discussion about the unintended harm being done to emergency aid operations by laws intended to target terrorists. The U.S. has put in place some of the most stringent counterterrorism laws and controls on humanitarian organizations globally. While recognizing the responsibility and necessity of protecting U.S. citizens and people around the world from acts of terror, these measures could have severe detrimental impacts on humanitarian operations if implemented to their full force in Syria. I urge you to support the Humanitarian Assistance Facilitation Act (HAFA) introduced in the House of Representatives late last year. This Act can help us to both safeguard against terror and save lives in Syria and in humanitarian crises elsewhere in the world. Humanitarian organizations need your help to safely operate in these contested and extremely dangerous contexts without the misperception of taking sides, or compromising the needs of conflict affected populations.

Counterterrorism laws have implications for aid operations not only inside Syria but also in Lebanon and elsewhere in the region.

4. U.S. policy should address the enormous burden and long-term challenges faced by Syria's neighbors

I commend the Governments of Lebanon, Jordan, Turkey, Iraq, and Egypt for their immense efforts in hosting millions of refugees. I urge the U.S. and Europe to respond with similar hospitality in terms of increased resettlement for Syrians. The U.N.'s Refugee Agency (UNHCR) aims to resettle over 100,000 Syrian refugees between 2015 and 2016. Syrians who need it should receive temporary protection outside of the Middle East.

Lebanon, in particular, has been extraordinarily generous in providing safety for families fleeing the horrors of the conflict. Lebanon is now the highest per capita refugee-hosting nation on earth. The crisis in Syria has cost the country more than $7.5bn, with municipal budgets, infrastructure and basic services facing total collapse. Jordanxix and Turkey have also been severally affected, as have Iraq and Egypt, which risk being forgotten by the world's media, donors, and governments.

There are millions of personal tragedies behind these statistics.

4.1 Growing harassment and exploitation

While most host communities are exceptionally welcoming of refugees, there are signs of growing discontentment and discrimination against people who have fled Syria's violence. They face increasingly severe restrictions on their ability to register as refugees, access basic services, earn an income, and receive protection from harassment and exploitation.

Host populations and refugees alike face rising food and rental prices, over-crowding in schools and increased competition for paid work. Daily labor wages in Lebanon and elsewhere have hit rock bottom. Refugees in Jordan are not allowed to work at all. Rental prices have risen 300 percent in some parts of Jordan, while 170,000 Lebanese have been pushed into poverty by the Syrian crisis. This risks further destabilization of the entire region.

Syrian families are increasingly pressing their young sons to work or their daughters into early marriage to support the family economically. I saw children as young as 5 packing fruit or picking vegetables, often for 8 hours or more a day, instead of going to school. Every 10th child is estimated to be working—often in dangerous conditions—while one in every five registered marriages of Syrian refugees in Jordan involves girls under the age of 18.

These are just some the problems Syrian children must routinely endure.

4.2 Finding homes and schools for children

As the conflict in Syria continues, children who have fled the fighting continue to miss out on an education—1.2 million children now live as refugees in host countries, but only half attend school, most often in overcrowded classrooms. Some of the Lebanese public schools I visited have more Syrian refugee children than Lebanese children attending their classes.

Syrian refugee children still tell me about their dreams of becoming teachers, carpenters, engineers, and doctors. They want to help their families and contribute positively to their society. We have a responsibility to give them the chance to fulfill their dreams. To prevent the loss of an entire generation of children, much greater support is urgently needed to ensure there are adequate schools and teachers for the millions of Syrian children and children in host communities in need of an education. Informal tuition and vocational training programs provided by NGOs are essential programs which require the support of governments so these children can become positive members, even future leaders, of their society. We cannot forget that one day they will lead the rebuilding of their country.

Parents struggle not only to cover the cost of schoolbooks, tuition, and transport; they are increasingly unable to afford homes for their families to live in.

On a recent visit I heard stories of countless families facing eviction and growing debt. I met some Palestinian families in Lebanon who had fled the fighting in Syria a year ago. After long and dangerous journeys—often in the dark, with small children and only some bags of clothes—they finally managed to cross into Lebanon. All other borders were closed to them. Eventually, shelter was found for them in small, one-room flats that the Norwegian Refugee Council was able to add to existing, crowded homes in preexisting Palestinian refugee camps. As additional families keep coming across the border to escape the violence in Syria, refugees already living in Lebanon have had to share their meagre accommodation with the new arrivals. Some families are now living 10 or 12 to a room.

The lack of affordable shelter in Jordan and Lebanon is an alarming problem. More than 80 percent of refugees live outside formal refugee camps, often residing in rundown and overcrowded flats, rudimentary structures, tents, or in abandoned or partially constructed buildings. With hundreds of thousands of refugees unable to repay debts or afford rising rental prices, large parts of the Middle East face an unprecedented housing crisis that requires your urgent attention.

Addressing this housing crisis will not be easy. The governments of Lebanon and Jordan require significant technical and financial support to help them develop more comprehensive shelter strategies. These strategies need your backing to ensure more homes are available on the market and rental price inflation is tackled.

The growing social and economic problems in countries hosting refugees can create pressure to close borders to new refugees fleeing Syria or introduce forced encampment.

4.3 Keeping borders open

Neighboring countries have absorbed a huge burden on behalf of the international community. The solidarity shown toward the Syrian refugees is admirable. Whilst it is difficult to ask, we need your help to ensure borders remain open to refugees—including Palestinians who face systematic discrimination. The creation of so-called "safe zones" and camps along the Syrian side of borders could be a recipe for increased violence against civilians, making matters worse, not better, for Syrian men, women, and children.

Governments beyond the region, including in the U.S., must also significantly increase the number of refugees they are willing to host or resettle to ease the pressure on neighboring countries. The meagre responses from nearly all Western nations, including my native country Norway, are simply not good enough. Media

48

reports suggest that at least 135,000 Syrians have applied for asylum in the United States. However, the current immigration policies have kept almost all of them out.

To help keep borders open and share the overwhelming burden, countries neighboring Syria will need both short- and long-term financial assistance.

4.4 Meeting long- and short-term needs

The United Nations has launched the largest appeal in its history, for $6.5bn. This sounds like a vast amount of money, but it is the same as Harvard University is asking for in its current fundraising drive. To date, only 12.5 percent of the U.N. appeal has been funded. Furthermore, this appeal does not include the millions more needed to fund cross-border humanitarian operations.

The United States and ordinary Americans have given extremely generously and this assistance has provided protection and life-saving aid for millions of Syrians. I would like to thank you for your efforts in this regard. Yet, with the region becoming increasingly unstable and the number of refugees expected to almost double by the end of 2014, even more resources will be needed. I am therefore asking you to dig even deeper and to consider all options, including pressing for greater backing from gulf donors and international financial institutions.

4.5 Supporting refugee-hosting governments

As an experienced humanitarian, I have seen that the average refugee crisis lasts more than a decade. And there is no end in sight to the fighting in Syria. When it does end, reconstruction will likely take decades. We will likely be responding to the Syria crisis for the next generation.

In order to deal with Syria's ''protracted crisis,'' U.S. and other donors will need to provide much-needed emergency response together with longer term development and macroeconomic assistance. Years of experience demonstrate that this must be done in parallel to ensure that immediate needs are met and that refugees and host communities have sustained access to health, education, and other services as well as viable livelihoods.

This comprehensive approach will require support by the international financial institutions, and much greater support to national development frameworks such as Jordan's national resilience plan and Lebanon's stabilization plan. It will also require greater funding to local authorities providing housing, access to health, water, education, and employment to both poor local people and refugees across the region.

The task at hand for the U.S. Government and the entire international community is therefore not only to meet the obligation set by the U.N. appeals—though this will remain critical. It is also to help support those communities and governments that will continue to bear the brunt of the refugee crisis for years to come.

If we do not act now to protect the region's future, the fallout from this conflict will be felt for generations.

CONCLUSION

The humanitarian free-fall experienced in Syria and across the region over the past 3 years must end now. Syria is testing our commitment to ensure the horrors of Srebrenica and Rwanda are not repeated and so far we are failing.

As with the conflicts raging now in South Sudan, the Central African Republic, and elsewhere, which should not be forgotten, the United States has the opportunity, and responsibility, to show real leadership to end the suffering in Syria. Together with the international community, I urge you to ensure that the United States makes use of all peaceful means to ensure that those in urgent need can access humanitarian assistance using the most direct routes, that cease-fires are negotiated and respected, that Syria's neighbors receive the support they require to prevent a societal breakdown, and that a political solution to the conflict is found without further delay.

For the Syrians who have fled the violence and will be unable to return to their homes for years to come, the right kind of short- and long-term assistance is required for them and for the communities and countries that host them. The Syrian children I have met across the region demand to know; when will they return home, go back to school and be reunited with their families. The international community, led by the U.S., has an obligation to find the answers to these questions, and urgently.

If there is no hope for Syrian youth, we will all see a more unstable future. If there are no schools and no jobs or new homes, we will see fertile grounds for extremism, violence, and terrorism. It is therefore both in line with our values and our interests to act now to protect and assist civilians caught in the crossfire.

I would like to thank you again for inviting me to testify and would welcome any questions you may have.

The CHAIRMAN. Well, thank you all for your testimony, and there are many questions that are raised in my mind listening. So let me start with Dr. Kilcullen. I want to pick up where we left in your testimony.

So what are the options? Because even accepting your view that no one is winning—I personally did not think that I was suggesting anyone was winning. I just think the regime made advances from where it was at one point that has changed its calculus about whether or not it can sustain itself and its patrons' calculus as well.

What are some of the policy considerations that you think we should be considering in order to create the dynamic that can lead us to the political solution that we all seek?

Dr. KILCULLEN. I have five specific things to suggest. But to start with, I think that one of the observations that is worth making is that the policy goals that have animated our approach to date, I would argue, have actually not been overly ambitious. Rather, they have been too minimalist. And one of the reasons why we have had trouble rallying the Congress, allies, and the American people behind strong action is because what we have sought to do is to manage and contain the conflict rather than to end it. And people do not want to support such a minimal goal when the costs are very clear but the benefits are not necessarily so clear.

So I agree that our approach should be to pursue a negotiated solution. I think the chance that that will ever happen without us telegraphing an intent and a willingness to use military force in order to generate that peaceful solution is next to zero. So I think that we should prefer indirect means where possible, but indirect means will not necessarily get us to the point where the regime feels that it has no option but to talk.

As I interpret the Syrian regime's strategy at this point, I believe that the regime is using the Geneva II process to buy time while it ramps up its military operations, tries to get into a better military situation ahead of the June elections, and then use the June elections to cement the regime for another term. And the reason that it is slow rolling on the handover of chemical weapons is the regime is currently the guarantor of those chemical weapons not falling into dangerous hands. If it gives up the chemical weapons, it loses that leverage and then there is no reason why we would keep the dialogue going with the Syrian regime. So they want to preserve the chemical weapons until such time as the election can take place, and then they will be set up for another period in office.

So my first recommendation should be that we should just ignore those June elections. We should say, yes, we know you have scheduled these elections. They are null and void. They are illegitimate. They have no force. And if you do persist in going ahead and carrying out the elections, they will have no bearing on international policy. I completely agree with what Ambassador Patterson said earlier, that to try to hold the elections under the current circumstances would be a complete joke, and we need to emphasize up front that we are not going to accept those results.

The second option that I suggest is we need to start exploiting linkages with other issues, and in particular, I think that Russia's intervention in Ukraine and the Crimea creates an opportunity as well as a challenge here. In my written testimony, I have gone into some detail on the very significant numbers of fighters from the Caucasus and from the Ukrainian Crimea who are currently operating in Syria as part of number of groups that are fighting right now under the authority of the Islamic Front. And in addition, as I mentioned earlier, there is now an offensive that is very close to the edge of the Russian naval base in Tartus. So it is, in fact, not at all beyond the realms of possibility that with several hundred fighters from the Caucasus who may, at some point, decide to go home to Russia and with threats to Russia's position in Syria, that the invasion of Ukraine and the international isolation and the economic pain that the Russians are going to increasingly be feeling as a result of that is linked to their support for the Assad regime in Syria. And if we play that linkage correctly in a diplomatic sense, it is entirely possible that we may be able to convince the Russians to cease their active support for the regime and perhaps even convince the regime that a negotiated settlement is in its best interest.

I agree with Dr. Nasr that the Iranians are, in fact, a more important supporter of the regime, but one thing that the Russians provide that is extraordinarily critical is maintenance support on a limited number of precision guided munitions and other support for the helicopters and other air assets that the regime is currently using to carry out its barrel bombs. So if you want to stop the barrel bombing offensive and you want to limit the ability of the regime to use its air to punish the population, then in fact attacking the Russian support is a way to do that.

The third point—and I agree with Mr. Egeland on this—is we need to focus on peace-building at the local level. Included in my written testimony is a report that my teams on the ground in Syria produced over the past 4 months which shows that of the two sides negotiating in the Geneva II process, there was never greater than 12 percent of Syrian respondents in any of the surveys conducted who had any degree of belief in the legitimacy of either the regime or the Itlaf, the group that was negotiating on behalf of the rebels. So almost 9 out of 10 Syrians thought that the process in Geneva was a waste of time because they did not believe that the sides that were negotiating were legitimate. If we want a future negotiated settlement to work, we have to start building cross-sectarian and cross-community interests at the local level in achieving a peace settlement. It cannot be something that comes in on top.

The fourth recommendation is to expand significantly our assistance programs to the opposition across four dimensions, nonlethal technical support, humanitarian assistance, training and advisory support, and I believe lethal technical weapons systems.

So the first point is humanitarian assistance. While I agree that we should avoid politicizing humanitarian assistance, the fact is it has already been politicized by the regime. It is not us who is denying humanitarian assistance to people in regime-controlled areas. It is the regime who is denying basic human services to people in besieged areas and areas that are rebel-controlled. So to the extent that we can put a greater degree of humanitarian assistance into the country, that breaks the regime's stranglehold on the population that it is currently trying to deny access.

We have just seen a successful U.N. Office of the Coordinator for Humanitarian Affairs convoy go into the Qamishli area in northeastern Syria and deliver assistance to the population of a Kurdish majority region. We need to be enforcing humanitarian corridors, access of humanitarian convoys, and the transportation of humanitarian assistance to the community. That will have an effect that is not only of benefit to the community, but it will also help to undermine the regime's strategy.

Nonlethal technical support. Sorry.

The CHAIRMAN. I have given you all of my time to answer the question. So I will read the rest of the testimony, but I think those are essential points.

Before I turn to Senator Corker, Mr. Egeland, what countries— I listened to both what you said and in your written statement about United States prioritizing efforts to ensure unimpeded aid delivery into Syria. What countries are blocking delivery of cross-border humanitarian assistance and to the extent do we know why?

Mr. EGELAND. Well, there are many hurdles to get across the borders. The first and most difficult is the security concerns inside. We go into areas where there is cross-fire and we need to negotiate with multiple opposition groups when we go into the opposition-held areas where we do cross-border which rightfully constitutes cross-border relief.

But there are from the neighboring states a number of bureaucratic hurdles, registration hurdles, et cetera, that we should not meet when we try to help and assist civilians on the other side. And very few donors have basically come up front and said, of course, we do cross-border. We support it. We fund it. We help it. We push it. Now there is also a Security Council resolution clearing that, giving a legal basis

The CHAIRMAN. Senator Corker.

Senator CORKER. Thank you, Mr. Chairman, and thank you all for your outstanding testimony and for being here today.

Mr. Egeland, I appreciate what you are doing. I doubt there are many people on this committee that have not visited the refugee camps and seen the tremendous distress that people are going through. After a few trips, you get to recognize the same people, meet with them, and nothing is changing much except that I know you all are providing a tremendous service and I appreciate you doing what you do.

Dr. Kilcullen, we spent a lot of time today talking about the administration versus the opposition, the Assad regime versus the opposition. But the opposition, as we know, is what is creating over time the threat to the homeland here. And you spent a lot of time in Iraq. I know you helped us develop strategies there. And I wonder if you might help us. You did such a great job there, but think about now just the opposition on the ground and help us think about down the road how we are going to need to deal with that and the differing strategies that they are using there.

Dr. KILCULLEN. Thank you, Senator. That is a very, very important question and I think it lies behind our reluctance to use military force because we worry that should we successfully topple the regime, what comes next. And one of the concerns is that not only would we see the emergence of a potential terrorist safe haven in Syria, but we may see the expansion of foreign fighters coming out of the country to Europe and elsewhere.

On the foreign fighter question, there are between 10 and 12 times as many foreign fighters going into and out of Syria as we saw even at the height of the war in Iraq. So it is an incredibly large flow of foreign fighters. They come from all over north Africa, from Western and eastern Europe, from Southeast Asia. They come from, of course, across the wider Middle East.

When we look at the opposition specifically, there are two groups that I think have been primarily of concern to this committee. One is Jabhat al-Nusra, the official al-Qaeda affiliate in Syria. The other is the Islamic State of Iraq and the Levant, which is in fact a successor organization to Al Qaeda in Iraq.

Right now, ISIL, as we call it, is in fact, I think, on something of a back foot. And again, I have included this in my written testimony. But in September 2013 in the town of Aleppo, which is Syria's largest city, at the beginning of our period of detailed research on that city, ISIL controlled no districts in the area. By the end of the year, they controlled about a quarter of the city, and it looked particularly bad. It looked as if the Islamic State of Iraq and the Levant was going to take over a very leading role in the opposition. But three things have really changed that.

Firstly, ISIL has not done very much to fight the regime. In fact, they have spent a lot of their time taking over districts that are away from the front line that are weak because who are fighting the regime are, in fact, not there because they are busy fighting the regime.

Secondly, they have imposed some extraordinarily negative consequences on the population in the areas where they live, kidnappings, tortures, beheadings, public execution of children. All the sorts of things that we became all too familiar with from these guys in Iraq we are still seeing in the area of Syria, and that has generated a very significant pushback against them from the local community.

So in the last 2 months, we have seen their support crash from controlling a quarter of the town to controlling next to no areas within Aleppo. And in fact, the position of ISIL is that they have withdrawn to the area of Raqqah on the Euphrates River and then creating a fairly geographically defined safe haven that is in a strip along the riverbed on either side of this area, a very localized area and, frankly, not in any way challenged to remove that area in the event of a large-scale military operation.

I think that in terms of foreign fighters, as I mentioned earlier, there is a lot of Chechens and Caucasian and Crimean fighters, but there are also a lot of fighters from Western European countries carrying Western European passports who have the ability to move back into the homeland over time. And we know that al-Qaeda has sent a very senior member that used to be its leader in Iran into Syria specifically to recruit and train Western European foreign fighters to reinsert into the west.

So I think it is an area of extraordinary concern that we need to be focusing on, but I think it is probably not the best solution to say that the real problem is ISIL and Jabhat al-Nusra. The real problem is the regime, and in fact, if we can create a more stable and peaceful environment in Syria, it is not beyond the realms of possibility that a significant number of fighters particularly within Jabhat al-Nusra would reintegrate within that process. I do not regard Jabhat al-Nusra as being in any way in the same category as ISIL.

Senator CORKER. I want to chase that in a minute, but I want to make sure we get to Dr. Nasr, and I do not know if we are going to have another round or not. But I appreciate you being here and I appreciate the time we spent yesterday elaborating a little bit on what you were going to say today and hearing more about it.

I wonder, for the committee, if you would talk a little bit about the shuttle diplomacy and what that actually means versus another Geneva-type conference and who the players would be, what you would think we want those players to try to achieve, or what we would want to achieve with them over a period of time.

Dr. NASR. Well, Senator, first of all, referring to what Dr. Kilcullen was saying, part of the problem of extremism is the support that goes from some of our allies toward groups that we would categorize as extremists or undesirable. I think, first of all, we would like our diplomacy to be directed toward this issue, namely where the funding for the fighters go, what might be the strategy for either both the moderate political force and the fighters that we want to see actually gain ground within Syria. There is a gap between the objectives of Qatar, Saudi Arabia, Turkey, and to some extent Iraq, politicians that they support and fund, groups within the opposition they back, and also the fighting groups on the ground that they give money to.

So our shuttle diplomacy, first and foremost, should be directed at creating some kind of a common position among these regional powers around what the end game in Syria is, who they back, and actually work with them to create a credible opposition. I mean, the fact that the opposition does not have the support on the ground, does not have credibility with the infighting that it has had, in the eyes of the regime also, it does not have credibility and uniformity.

Secondly, I think all the regional actors have an interest in the fighting to come to an end. Even I think Iran's position is very different from Russia's because largely Iran is also suffering a loss of status in the region. It is fairly expensive for the Iranian Government to invest in supporting the Assad regime given the pressure of sanctions and the economic issues that they have. There is an incentive to find some kind of a solution out there.

The United States does not deal with Iran, but the United Nations does and also some of the regional allies do. For instance, Turkey and Qatar are dealing with Iran on a variety of these issues.

But ultimately a political settlement would require that the Iranians decide that it is not worth supporting Assad, that there might be solutions around Assad and without Assad in Syria and that the Turks, Saudis, and the Qataris agree to a political force that would be taking over in Syria in some capacity when Assad goes. I mean, currently if you looked at it, even if Assad left, there is no agreement on the other side what the successor regime would look like and who would take over. You are going to have immediately a confrontation between Turkey, Saudi Arabia, and Qatar as to whose clients will dominate a post-Assad scenario there. And so I think we have to put our shoulder to creating some kind of a framework, a basic framework, at least among our allies as a starting point which could provide some kind of credibility for a diplomatic process.

Senator CORKER. I know it is time for someone else to ask questions. I know you know this and I know you know it better probably than anybody up here, but we had sort of that strategy in the beginning. We were going to work with the neighborhood. And it appears to me the reason the neighborhood split was we never delivered on our side, and so they all went their own way, again because we said what we were going to do. We did not do it. People split apart. Now they are supporting different groups that are warring with each other. But you believe we can put that back together with the appropriate amount of effort.

Dr. NASR. Well, I fully agree with you. I think we gave a signal to the neighborhood that we are going to take care of this crisis and then we did not. And then when the neighborhood witnessed that we were not participating in the crisis—and also I agree with you that through the chemical weapons deal, essentially we turned Assad into a partner in an international agreement that requires his acquiescence. The region decided that they have to take care of their own interests on their own. So they began funding different groups. They do not have a mechanism for cooperation. I think Egypt's solid relations between Turkey, Qatar, and Saudi Arabia— in some ways Syria is paying a price for what happened in Egypt, and therefore we have now a much more complicated situation.

I actually do not think it is as simple as we think in terms of changing the military calculus on the ground anymore or necessarily to fix it ourselves with shifting certain strategies. We have to deal with the fact that the region has now invested heavily in the future of Syria. They view this as a zero sum game, and this requires a diplomatic effort of rolling back this involvement. We have to gain the trust of the region that actually we mean business, that this time we are going to deliver, that we are not going to come up with grandiose solutions for the region but rather actually start by listening to the actors in the region in terms of what they see and try to work to get them to talk to one another and come up with a position that we could then support.

Senator CORKER. Thank you.

The CHAIRMAN. Senator Kaine.

Senator KAINE. Dr. Nasr, just to continue on that line of thought, your written testimony says that the region, quote, "lacks any regional mechanism that would allow regional actors to solve this conflict." Now, this is thinking way down the road, but "regional mechanism"—what kind of a mechanism are you envisioning or should be in place, should be part of a long-term strategy for future conflicts here?

Dr. NASR. Well, I mean, if you looked at this region, as troubled as it is, it does not have anything equivalent to an ASEAN or Organization of American States or Organization of African Union. It has an Arab League, but the two biggest other players in Syria, Turkey, and Iran, do not belong to the Arab League. And for a very long time, the United States has played a very important role in this region in terms of coordinating relations between countries, filling the vacuum when the region itself has not been able to address its problems. And all of a sudden, I think in the past 4 or 5 years, we have backed away from playing that role in the region. And, therefore, you are seeing that the region cannot cope with an issue like Syria. There is no conversation—actually Syria's conversation going around in the region around how do you bring even a cease-fire to Syria. Let us even forget about Iran. Among our allies, there is not a conversation.

Senator KAINE. Is it your opinion that the U.S. activity in the past in the region has been in lieu of a regional mechanism or has it actually been harmful to the creation of a regional mechanism?

Dr. NASR. Well, we could say that we never actually really invested in creating a mechanism like we did in other parts of the world, but in reality, it is we are where we are and creating mechanisms going forward I think is useful to the region. It is the best way of allowing us to leave the region. But as Syria shows, a sudden U.S. lack of interest in a major regional issue could be quite devastating because it actually worsens the problem. Syria has suffered because of American neglect. It has become a larger problem, which I think down the road will exact a higher cost from us to solve than had we paid attention to it 2 years ago when it was less complicated.

Senator KAINE. Is the Arab League capable of being that mechanism? Is it capable of ever gaining significant participation by Turkey or Saudi Arabia, or is that just not possible for a variety of cultural or other reasons?

Dr. NASR. Well, Turkey is not a member of the Arab world.

Senator KAINE. I understand.

Dr. NASR. They are not in.

Senator KAINE. But even as a partner, we have non-NATO members that are partners with NATO.

Dr. NASR. That is possible down the road. But the bigger problem right now is that the two biggest Arab participants in Syria, both of whom are Arab, have opened a cold war between them. I mean, Saudi Arabia engineered an expulsion of Qatar from GCC, which is quite significant given that GCC was supposed to be the main anti-Iran containing mechanism in the Persian Gulf region. It has been broken up.

Senator KAINE. And that cold war—and this is helpful to me. That cold war is exacerbated by Syria but not purely caused by the situation in Syria. Correct?

Dr. NASR. Well, it was actually caused largely by Egypt, by a major disagreement over the fate of President Morsi's government. But Syria is where the disagreement is playing out in a very lively manner.

Senator KAINE. I may have missed this when I was voting, but talk a little bit about the role of Hezbollah in Syria. I think your testimony—I cannot remember which testimony was about 3,000 to 5,000 Hezbollah fighters from Lebanon into Syria, and that has created huge challenges in Lebanon. In the pantheon of support for the Assad regime, Iran, Russia, Hezbollah, what has been the impact of Hezbollah's support?

Dr. KILCULLEN. I will pick that up, Senator. That was in my testimony.

So I fully agree with you in your take on the effect of Hezbollah ramping up its operations in Syria on the situation in Lebanon. Hezbollah has had a reputation of protecting both Sunni and Shia communities against, for want of a better term, infidel groups, and it has had a reputation for being focused on putting Lebanon first. That is now in tatters because it sent about 5,000 fighters to the western part of Syria where they have been participating in some of the most significant regime offenses that have no benefit to the Lebanese people but have, of course, benefited their ally in Syria.

In addition, there are specialist units working as advisors and leaders with not so much the regular Syrian forces but with the Syrian National Defense Forces, which is the unified group of all the irregular and militia fighters that, until he was killed on the weekend, worked under President Assad's cousin.

The Hezbollah participation I think is important because not only are the numbers significant, 5,000 fighters, but also because these are people who have a lot of experience in urban irregular warfare against Israel and against other players, and they have brought a lot of those skills to bear in training and lifting the capability of the Syrian forces that they are working with. Hezbollah is a small but important player.

Senator KAINE. Dr. Kilcullen, you say that the reputation for putting Lebanon first and being a little bit of a protector of both Sunni and Shia is in tatters. Is there any indication that you have seen or that anybody on the panel has seen that suggests that Hezbollah's political influence is being degraded within Lebanon because of this decision to go all in with Assad in Syria?

Dr. KILCULLEN. I will defer to my colleagues.

I would just offer one observation up front which is that we saw Hassan Nasrallah, the head of Hezbollah, actually make an appeal on Lebanese television last year to say, look, we know that we do not like each other. We are in Syria. We are going to be in Syria. If we hate each other, let us kill each other in Syria instead of here in Lebanon. For a guy who was the cock of the walk at the end of the war against Israel in 2006, was in an extraordinarily dominant political position through 2007 and 2008, for him now to be reduced to basically begging off a fight against his political foes in Lebanon I think is suggestive of how damaging it has been.

But I will defer to the others.

Senator KAINE. Other thoughts on that question?

Dr. NASR. I think the mood has changed. I think Hezbollah's rhetoric is much more self-confident and bullish than it was a year ago. It very much sort of tracks with Assad's rhetoric. I think the way Nasrallah has pitched this is that if the Sunnis won in Syria, then Lebanon would be next, and the best way of protecting the Shias' position in Lebanon was to keep Assad where he is or at least prevent Assad from falling. I think they have achieved that.

I think mostly the Iranian and the Hezbollah position is not that they are going to give a knockout blow and actually win in Syria, but because the perception was that Assad was going to fall for a very long time in the next 2 months and he has not, by just staying in the fight, they basically have the fight both regional and international expectations. And that gives them an aura of the glass being half full rather than being half empty.

Senator KAINE. One last point. I just want to thank Mr. Egeland. I was in Lebanon recently, and the NRC folks were very helpful and I was very impressed with their work.

What did, Mr. Egeland, you and Dr. Nasr think? Dr. Kilcullen was, I think, at least a little provocative compared to some of what I have heard by starting his testimony challenging the notion that the regime is winning. He pointed out that 75 percent of the country is now not controlled by the regime, and he put appropriate caveats on that. But I just am curious as to each of your thoughts. Is his challenging of the notion that the regime is winning—do you see it the same way or do you see it in a different way?

Dr. NASR. I think technically, factually Dr. Kilcullen is right, but politics also is about perception. And I think in the perception game, Iran, Hezbollah, Assad are doing better than they were a year and a half ago, 2 years ago. For instance, the Prime Minister of Turkey multiple times said Assad will be gone within 2 months. He is still there. And I think that basically among their ranks translates into having been able to withstand the worst of it. They are still standing, and it is more a perception than the fact. So I think Dr. Kilcullen is right, but we have to take that dimension into account, particularly when people come to a negotiating table. Are they coming feeling there is wind in their sails or are they feeling deflated and defeated?

Mr. EGELAND. If I may say, as a humanitarian, the following. There is a strong sense that everybody is losing. Nobody is winning, and especially the civilian population is losing more and more. There are now, I think, 2,000 opposition groups with a name. There is very much a stalemate in very many places except internal battles on either side, all making international or national local relief work very difficult. And the total disregard for human rights, humanitarian law of armed conflict, for the rights of civilians for basic principles like sparing the wounded, sparing civilians, women and children, safe passage is not really there.

However, I would say that one of the reasons that we are—I think Dr. Kilcullen said, I mean, we are losing the public on this. I have been an aid worker now, a humanitarian, for 30 years. We do not have the popular engagement as we had during the Bosnia period or Rwanda period and so on. And I think the wrong narrative many have is that it is bad guys against bad guys. So why should I be involved? I think the right way of seeing this is it is bad guys against very good civilians, and we need to help these civilians. You know, civilians down there are being kicked out.

Of course, there are also very honorable people fighting there, but first and foremost, it is a lot of civilians and we can help them. We do help them all the time. You should be proud of U.S. money going to keep up a very, very significant humanitarian effort. If we had not had it, hundreds of thousands would have died. And the resolution that you, Senator Kaine, and Senator Rubio has introduced helps us in this because it is a question of lack of access. We need access. We have a right of access, and they have a right to receive our assistance.

The CHAIRMAN. Well, this has been very helpful.

I just have one final set of questions to tie all of this testimony together in my own mind.

So, Dr. Nasr, in your testimony, your recommendations—basically what you have voiced here is the United States and its European allies should focus diplomatic attention on bringing Saudi, Qatari, and Turkish positions on Syria into alignment, unifying the Syrian opposition and laying the groundwork for a regional diplomatic framework for ending the war in Syria.

Now, is it possible to bring the allies into alignment without ultimately part of that changing the military equation? Are they not out of alignment because they came to the conclusion that we were not going to do what was necessary to get rid of Assad and therefore they took it upon their own, understanding their individual interests? And I am not condoning some of the actions that our allies have taken here. But the question is how does one bring them into alignment unless they know that there is a plan in which you are going to ultimately achieve changing the battlefield equation to then create the political dynamic as you are working to unify the Syrian opposition.

Dr. NASR. I think, Senator, your point is well taken. I think something worse than not having a military strategy is that everybody on the ground believes that you do not have it. And I think we have gone out of our way to convince everybody that we do not have a military strategy and we do not want one. I think at the time of the chemical weapons agreement, we made a very strenuous case for why we were not going to contemplate any kind of military action. I think you are correct that everybody in the region understood exactly what we were saying and therefore took matters into their own hands.

I approach this testimony realistically, that I do not see any evidence of a change of heart on the military question. So considering that we are not going to go out there and argue that we are willing to actually have some kind of a military threat on the ground, the next best thing is to change at least the existing diplomatic scenario. There could be a far more credible diplomatic approach which could also be construed in some ways as not changing the facts on the ground, the military reality on the ground, but changing, if you would, the diplomatic, now very comfortable diplomatic, scenario in which the Assad regime operates. So having Russia as a partner creates a situation in which Syria is protected internationally in a major way. You have to put Russia aside.

The CHAIRMAN. Let me refine this then. How would you get the allies that you referred to in your testimony to be aligned with us if they do not feel that ultimately Assad will be out of the picture?

Dr. NASR. Well, actually because we have not had a policy for a long time and they do have a policy, it is more getting them to be aligned with one another and for us to commit that we will be aligned with a sensible policy that they develop. I do not think anybody is going to be basically very quickly abandoning their own positions in order to array behind the United States unless we are going to basically take over this conflict. So largely it is that they already have policies on the ground, and it is possible to get them to, for instance, back one set of actors within the Syrian opposition around a single platform to begin to coordinate their funding on the ground around a particular set of groups and around a particular objective, both militarily and politically, and then the United States would make a commitment that it is going to support what that platform would be.

The CHAIRMAN. Dr. Kilcullen, I cut you off because my time had expired, and I am reading your testimony, point number 5, plan for limited military strikes. And you have caveats in there about what you mean by that, but could you synthesize that for the record here for me?

Dr. KILCULLEN. Yes, sir. I wanted to say that we can do a limited amount of very good work by supporting the opposition, but at some point, we need to start taking the regime down if we are going to change the correlation of forces. So when we talk about the military calculus on the ground, what we are really talking about is numbers. So in terms of forces, the regime right now has something between about 200,000 and 340,000 troops of all kinds in the field, including both foreign fighters who have come to support the regime and the irregulars and the regime's own troops. The rebels have about 200,000 at most. So neither side has the sort of 3-to-1 classic advantage that you would expect in a conventional fight as a precursor to victory. The regime is certainly nowhere close to the roughly 10-to-1 ratio that we expect in a counterinsurgency environment.

There is no way that the regime can win. But as President Assad said, they think they can. They have the wind behind them. They have a degree of confidence that is actually unfounded. So it is very important that we convince the regime that they actually cannot win, and I believe that to do that, we need to telegraph our willingness to use direct military force, not just indirectly supporting the rebels.

So what I have suggested in my written testimony is the idea of a campaign of roughly the size of Kosovo or of being a fight protector in Libya, so predominantly an air campaign. I would not rule out a limited number of specialist personnel, whether civilian or military, on the ground to assist in targeting and directing of air strikes. But I suggest that what we want to do is craft a campaign around the idea of protecting at-risk civilians in safe zones, creating no-fly areas to deny the kinds of barrel bombing attacks that we are seeing, and establishing humanitarian corridors to allow civilians to move to those safe zones, and particularly targeting critical regime capabilities, air, artillery, long-range rockets, chemical weapons perhaps to convince the regime that its best option is to negotiate an end to the conflict, most likely via a transitional government under international supervision.

Extremist groups that sought to undermine that kind of peaceful solution would then become legitimate targets of a subsequent phase of that operation. So it is not a question of taking down the regime only to see extremist groups step into its place. It is about creating the conditions in which the regime comes to the table knowing that it has to talk because that is its best option.

I should emphasize that military operations are never predictable. The outcome is always in doubt, and it sometimes looks clean and simple but it never is. So I am very conscious that this is perhaps an extreme suggestion, but I think if we are not at least thinking about this and at least planning for it, it is extraordinarily unlikely that the regime will ever see us as being strong enough to be worth talking to, even in a diplomatic sense.

Effectively my view of what happened last September was that we called our own bluff. We said we were going to strike. The regime did what we said was crossing the redline. We did not strike at that time. If we are going to have any leadership role in a future diplomatic engagement, we need to reestablish that credibility, and at this point I am afraid I do not think that is possible without showing the willingness to use force.

The CHAIRMAN. Finally, Mr. Egeland, it struck me when in your oral testimony you said in 30 years of humanitarian work, that this is the worst set of circumstances that you have seen. I can imagine 30 years' worth of work and some of the challenges that have existed and the humanitarian crises that existed in the world. That is an incredibly strong and profound statement. Why do you say that this is the worst?

Mr. EGELAND. Because of the sheer scale really—6.5 million displaced inside plus more than 2.5 million outside. Nine million people have been driven out of their homes, another 3 million in absolute miserable situations as war victims inside. So that is 12 million people. But even the Balkans was never like that with 12 million people in that kind of a situation.

Of course, in the central African region, many more people were killed, but not even there either were there 12 million people who had the lives devastated.

So I really have struggled with how to get the message out to people, to parliaments, to journalists or policymakers that it does not get bigger than this.

On your call here in Congress, it has not gotten bigger anytime and it will not probably. And at the same time, I have the hope that we can change it. We can provide hope to these children. I mentioned this Myriam who wants to be a doctor. The children of Syria have not given up. It is not like they want to flock to extremism. They hope to become teachers. And that is the narrative we have to get through. It is huge, this thing, and we can change it.

The CHAIRMAN. Senator Corker.

Senator CORKER. Just two questions. And again, thank you all for your testimony. I think it has been very enlightening.

When you said extreme relative to the military option, I do not think it is extreme. I just think that we missed the opportunity when the opportunity was right, and I agree with you. We called our own bluff, and I think we hurt ourselves tremendously not just in Syria but candidly in other parts of the world.

So I do not think it is going to happen that way. I do not think there is going to be a military option, and I think all three of us here supported the AUMF and hoped that at the window in time, that very short involvement that was going to degrade significantly was going to happen.

But as you mentioned, Mr. Egeland, I mean, the country obviously was in a different place at that time. There was not a case made for it in fairness, and there is not a case being made for the humanitarian crisis that is happening there.

But just as a humanitarian, when you hear potentially about a military option that is not likely to occur now—I think that time has come and gone—how does that affect you? I mean, when you see the crisis there, do you think it is something that warrants some type of activity in that regard to change the dynamic as a humanitarian?

Mr. EGELAND. As humanitarians, we do not call for military action. Of course, there is under the rubric of the responsibility to protect, agreed by heads of states from all of the U.N., that military means is the last resort when there are no other options.

I personally think we can do as an international community more diplomatically, politically, humanitarian-wise, sanctions-wise, in many ways. And I agree with Dr. Nasr. One can put leverage on the sponsors and suppliers on all sides to try to avoid the escalations that we have seen every single month now for a very long time. And those supporting the government side are always referring to supplies coming to the other side, and those on the other side, the supplies coming to the government side. It can easily become an arms race and the civilians in the middle, and we who are the suppliers of humanitarian relief come in the middle. But I would not rule out anything.

What we are asking for in the cross-border and so on is, of course, that even the cross-border thing is sort of hush-hush. We do not want to provoke anybody. I think one should go massively across the Turkish, Iraqi, Jordanian borders to civilians in great need, and it should be facilitated by the donors. It should be facilitated by neighboring countries, and there is a Security Council resolution on the table, and even that is not happening.

Senator CORKER. And facilitated with security forces making that happen. Is that what I am hearing you say?

Mr. EGELAND. No. As I say in my statements, I mean, the border crossings frequently are not open, and I am talking about neighboring states even. Those groups on the inside that are supported by gulf countries are not really helping us very often and they could. There is too little funding for these operations. They are not coordinated well. The U.N. is not behind it or pushing or helping this because they are on the government side. So that will be a very easy way to say we can reach millions of people in that simple way, and it does not need military force.

Senator CORKER. Mr. Chairman, I have a lot of questions. I saw Dr. Kilcullen looking at his watch. I have a feeling he has a 5 o'clock appointment. So I am going to stop. I thank you, and we are going to follow up with both of you by telephone. Thank you.

The CHAIRMAN. Well, I appreciate it. The insights of this panel have been extraordinarily helpful.

I will say, as I was listening to your response, Mr. Egeland, to Senator Corker, that our way to create pressure with other countries is either, to the extent that they are subject to being moved by international opinion, that will make them act in certain ways, that is one way. The other ways are when we use our aid and our trade to induce them to act in a certain way. The third way is when we deny them our aid or our trade or have another arsenal of what we would call economic sanctions. And after that, there is not much left to use in the arsenal of peaceful diplomacy tools.

And so we are talking about Russia and Iran here as two patrons and entities engaged and involved in the Syria issue. I can just see as we are negotiating with the Iranians on their nuclear weapons program that when we lift the sanctions on them, they will have a lot more money and a lot more resources to continue to be engaged in Syria. So these are some of the challenges that we face when we are thinking about this broader question.

But I appreciate all of your work, all of your insights.

And this record will remain open until the close of business tomorrow.

And with the gratitude of the committee, this hearing is adjourned.

[Whereupon, at 5 p.m., the hearing was adjourned.]

ADDITIONAL MATERIAL SUBMITTED FOR THE RECORD

RESPONSES OF AMBASSADOR ANNE PATTERSON TO QUESTIONS
SUBMITTED BY SENATOR ROBERT MENENDEZ

Question. What is the worst case outcome for the Syrian war? What is the best case? In which direction is the current state of affairs trending?
- Based on this assessment, are there specific areas of U.S. policy that the admin- istration is reevaluating in order to increase the likelihood that we can avoid a worst-case scenario?

Answer. Circumstances in Syria continue to deteriorate. While we regularly reexamine and challenge the core assumptions that inform our policymaking process, the administration has not changed its fundamental policy on Syria. Our goals remain to: (1) counter violent extremism and prevent the establishment of a terrorist safe-haven in Syria; (2) avoid the collapse of the Syrian state and its institutions; (3) prevent the transfer or use of chemical weapons (CW); (4) support and bolster the security of Syria's neighbors; (5) alleviate humanitarian suffering resulting from the conflict; and (6) help foster a negotiated transition leading to a representative government that is responsive to the needs of the Syrian people.

We continue to believe that the Assad regime is a magnet for terrorism and that the best, most durable resolution to the conflict is a mutually agreed-upon political transition. We are considering a range of policy tools that would bring us closer to achieving this transition.

Question. How has the regime's recapture of Yabroud and ongoing infighting among opposition groups in northern Syria affected the prospects for each side in the conflict?

Answer. The regime's recapture of Yabroud was undoubtedly a setback for the opposition forces, but this is a bloody war of attrition and we do not believe it can be resolved on the battlefield.

We continue to encourage the moderate opposition, both political and armed, to be more unified, to coordinate more effectively, and to build better connections with civilian Syrian populations. I would cite the Syrian Opposition Coalition's (SOC) expected visit to Washington, DC, in the coming months as evidence that the moderate opposition has made strides in that direction. Nevertheless, the degree to which the moderate opposition continues to face challenges in coalescing around a shared political platform is a distraction from its efforts to rid Syria of violent extremists and a despotic regime.

Question. In your testimony, you said that "we are reviewing our policy and identifying priorities for coordination action." What is the status of this policy review? Will you consult with Congress on the priorities you identify for coordinated action?

Answer. The process to which I referred is ongoing and fluid, as is the conflict itself. We are not currently in a position to brief the Congress on any new policy shift or initiative, but if, and when, any new steps are pursued, the administration will consult with Congress.

Question. Despite working admirably and in good faith to seek a political solution to end the violence in Syria, the Syrian opposition has had difficulty building broad support among communities inside Syria.

♦   (a) What is the U.S. doing to help the Syrian opposition build

legitimacy? Answer. Through senior-level meetings and other symbolic—but

important—acts,

we are attempting to help the SOC effectively represent the aspirations of the Syrian people. We expect to receive a senior SOC delegation in Washington, DC, in May, during which we hope to have productive discussions that further deepen our cooperation and understanding of one another.

We also seek to strengthen the SOC through our foreign assistance programs, which encourage it to strengthen ties with communities inside Syria. In this vein, we have successfully facilitated multiple SOC meetings with local councils, media outlets, and grassroots organizations over the past year.

We continue to provide assistance to local councils across Syria, an initiative implemented in close coordination with SOC's Assistance Coordination Unit (ACU). Our assistance helps the ACU strengthen its ability to respond to the needs of Syrians and conduct outreach inside Syria. With our help, the ACU has taken a lead role in determining the distribution of urgent equipment such as fire trucks, water bladders, ambulances, food baskets, and school supplies. The United States also provides operational support and resources to increase the SOC's connectivity to constituents, civil society, and local authorities, including funding to support their participation in the Geneva II process as well as outreach events such as townhall meetings, travel into Syria, and the establishment of satellite offices across Syria.

♦   (b) Does the administration still believe that the SOC has the credibility, capa- bility, and commitment to lead the post-Assad transition?

Answer. As an entity, the SOC does not seek, nor do we encourage it, to lead the post-Assad transition. Rather, we believe that an inclusive, representative, and capable political body like the SOC is needed to negotiate on the behalf of the Syrian people for the creation of a post-Assad transitional governing body. We assess that the SOC has the credibility, capability, and commitment to represent Syrians in these efforts. It has already taken important steps to coordinate efforts with other opposition groups and international partners. The SOC has started institutionalizing mechanisms to consult and cooperate more formally with the broad spectrum of Syrian society, all of which will be needed to make a transition succeed.

♦   (c) Are Syrian opposition forces receiving U.S. assistance capable of shifting the stalemate on the ground in Syria and pushing back both extremist groups and Assad's Iran and Russia-backed forces? Are fighters with the Free Syrian Army compliant with international humanitarian law and human rights standards?

Answer. Despite the asymmetry of forces on the ground, the opposition has been able to maintain and hold territory, even after 3 years of fighting. They spearheaded the initiative to fight extremists, even while continuing to fight the regime.

Nevertheless, we recognize that they are facing an uphill battle. We understand that our nonlethal assistance will not directly determine outcomes on the battlefield nor will it, on its own, force Assad to change his calculus about retaining power. However, our assistance does provide needed financial support, equipment, and supplies, while sending a signal both to those inside and outside Syria of our strong support for the moderate opposition.

The Supreme Military Council (SMC) has repeatedly reiterated to us its commitment to abiding by international law and the SOC has condemned the violations committed by opposition forces. I would be happy to refer you to SMC and SOC documents that affirm these commitments. Moreover, the USG supports the documentation of violations on all sides for future transitional justice measures.

♦   (d) The State Department's Bureau of Conflict and Stabilization Operations has been focused on helping to build ties between the Syrian opposition and commu- nities inside Syria. How does the CSO Bureau evaluate the effectiveness and progress in these programs?

Answer. In October 2013, CSO initiated an impact review after the first fiscal year (FY 2013) of its programming in support of the Syrian opposition. In FY 2014, CSO began conducting quarterly impact assessments of its programming in Syria. These assessments use a maturity model approach (a framework that sets benchmarks for comparison of progress) to evaluate effectiveness based on outcomes related to:

- Building cohesion of the moderate opposition (internally and externally);
  - Strengthening media and civil society linkages to prepare the Syrian people for a political transition; and
  - Promoting an inclusive, pro-democratic Syrian society that counters violent extremism (CVE).

Cohesion: Based on its analysis, CSO has determined that it has had some success increasing cohesion between the Syrian opposition and local communities inside Syria that it targets with its programming. Provincial-level coalitions are emerging (mainly in Northwest Syria) around consensus-based governance that seeks to provide real benefit and a voice to local communities. This can be seen in the expanding ties between local and provincial councils, the development of provincial-level structures for civil defense and policing, and in the slowly expanding ties between provinces.

Political Transition: After 40 years of regime-dominated media, CSO is working to foster a pro-democratic media network out of small, disparate activists, primarily through radio and TV. These media outlets—11 FM radio and two satellite television stations—aim to hold the regime, opposition, and extremists accountable for their actions; mobilize and inform local populations; and provide a conduit for the moderate opposition to reach wider audiences.

Inclusion/CVE: CSO's Syria programming seeks to (a) increase inclusion and empowerment of women, minorities, and other vulnerable groups; and (b) enable the moderate opposition and individual communities to more effectively resist extremism (largely through support to media and police forces). The capacity to resist extremism is particularly important as many of the groups CSO is working with are prime targets for extremist attacks as a result of their moderate political messaging and initiatives.

- ♦ (e) In your opening statement, you say that State and USAID have started to channel resources directly to local and provincial governments and civil society groups. Why are resources being sent directly rather than through the SOC?

Answer. U.S. nonlethal assistance to the Syrian opposition is closely coordinated with the Syrian Opposition Council's (SOC) Assistance Coordination Unit (ACU) to ensure that U.S. Government assistance is meeting emerging needs in Syria. In some instances, we have refocused our assistance to areas where moderates are maintaining control. In areas where extremists have been ejected, we have moved to boost moderates' ability to govern and provide basic services to fill the vacuum. Implementing this strategy necessitates that we sometimes engage directly with moderate and capable councils, and civil society groups, inside Syria that are in need of international support.

In addition to our coordination with the SOC and ACU in our overall assistance efforts, we provide assistance directly to these organizations. For instance, the SOC recently held its first outreach activity supported by U.S. funding, a large-scale gathering of activists and local council members from inside Syria. At the event, the SOC assured civil society and local authorities of its commitment to being inclusive, transparent, and engaged. The United States has also provided nearly $1 million in direct assistance to the ACU to support its operational, programmatic, and outreach capabilities. This type of assistance is critical to our larger policy goal of achieving a negotiated political solution that puts an end to the violence and ultimately leads to a representative government that is responsive to the needs of the Syrian people.

- ♦ (f) How does the administration view recent leadership disputes within the Supreme Military Council and what criteria will the administration use to assess the potential value of providing further support to armed opposition groups?

Answer. We view the recent ascendance of Gen. Abdul-Ilah al-Bashir as an attempt by the SMC to build stronger ties between the armed and political opposition, a goal that we have long supported.

We are in constant contact with opposition leaders in order to learn about the challenges faced by Syrian communities and consider their specific requests. We assess the value of our assistance according to the feedback we receive from opposition leaders and regular monitoring and evaluation practices.

Question. Assad has been spending unsustainably to fight this civil war. He has secured some financing in the shape of loans from Iran and barter contracts with

Russian banks exchanging Syrian oil for staple commodities but his financial reserves continue to dwindle as he spends more money that he takes in.

- How much money does Assad have left?
- Where is his outside funding coming from and what forms do that funding or assistance take?
- How is Assad sustaining operations in the face of dwindling reserves?
- You said in your testimony that the U.S. is working with members of the opposition, and other states in the region to cut off sources of funding and recruits for violent extremists in Syria. Please describe how the U.S. Government is doing this.

Answer. The United States is committed to increasing pressure on and isolating the Assad regime and its supporters until they recognize that the best resolution to this conflict is a negotiated political transition. The State Department, along with Treasury, is bringing significant diplomatic weight to bear in order to pressure companies around the world to cease their dealings with the Assad regime.

The combined effects of U.S. and international pressure and sanctions on Syria have placed a considerable toll on Assad's financial reserves and sources of funding. This pressure has forced the regime to take extraordinary steps—including harmful inflationary measures—to secure the funds that maintain its war effort, which it prioritizes over all else.

With respect to the activities of violent extremists, the U.S. Government leverages diplomatic engagement, information-sharing, technical assistance, and sanctions to cut off funding to extremists in Syria. The United States is working with countries in the region to strengthen their ability to detect and interdict financial flows to extremists. The United States has also designated several key terrorist financiers and facilitators, effectively cutting off their access to the U.S. financial system.

Multilateral diplomacy will also continue to be crucial in the context of preventing and interdicting foreign extremist travel to and from Syria. We are working with members of the opposition, Syria's neighbors, and other regional states to interdict and encourage prosecution of these extremists, cut off their financial resources, and prevent radicalization and recruitment to their cause. Ambassador Robert Bradtke, the Department of State's Senior Advisor for Partner Engagement on Syria Foreign Fighters, is leading the Department and interagency efforts in engaging foreign partners on this issue.

Question. Our partners in the Gulf Cooperation Council (GCC) are supporting elements of the Syrian Opposition and providing humanitarian aid, nonlethal and lethal assistance. Saudi Arabia has reportedly been in talks with Pakistan to purchase man-portable antiaircraft (MAN–Pad) and antitank missile systems, which the administration has objected to as recently as February.

- Are you satisfied by the level of coordination on Syria with GCC partners?
- Is coordination better with some GCC members? If so, which countries are more difficult to coordinate with? How can the U.S. improve its coordination with GCC members on Syria?
- What is your view on the provision of missile systems to Syrian opposition groups?

Answer. As we focus and improve our own assistance channels, we are working more closely with regional partners to maximize the impact of our collective assistance. We share a common understanding with our gulf partners regarding the importance of ensuring that violent extremists not benefit from external assistance. We will continue to improve coordination through regular consultations with our partners.

We have not changed our position on providing missile systems to the Syrian opposition. We continue to have concerns about the attendant proliferation risk that could provide terrorist groups with the capability to threaten civilian aviation.

Question. The Russian state arms manufacturer Rosoboronexport has been the Pentagon's supplier of Mi-17 helicopters to the Afghan National Security Forces (ANSF) but has also been selling arms to the Assad regime. Some have advocated for cancelling our contracts with Rosoboronexport and sanctioning the company for Russia's annexation of Crimea.

- (a) What military equipment has the Assad regime acquired from Rosoboron- export? How has the quantity and quality of Russian weapons shipments to Syria changed over the last 3 years? Over the last few months?

Answer. The answer was submitted under separate cover to the Chairman (prepared by INR).

◆ (b) Would sanctions on Rosoboronexport related to Ukraine impact Assad? If so, how?

Answer. Rosoboronexport is a Russian state-owned arms exporter involved in Russian international arms trade to Syria. As you know, U.S. involvement with Rosoboronexport exists primarily to meet an urgent need to field Mi-17 military-use helicopters for the Afghan National Security Forces (ANSF). While any U.S. sanctions on Rosoboronexport regarding events in Ukraine would likely impact Rosoboronexport's overall operations, it may not directly impact the company's dealings with Syria.

The President has announced a series of measures that will continue to increase the cost to Russia for its actions in Ukraine. The President's Executive Orders 13660, 13661, and 13662 authorize sanctions on individuals or entities involved in certain prohibited actions, including entities operating in the defense and related materiel sector in the Russian Federation. This authority is currently being used as part of a calibrated response to the Russian actions in Ukraine. The administration continues to be committed to resolving the situations in both Ukraine and Syria.

◆ (c) Under the current contract with Rosoboronexport, how many Mi-17s have been delivered to the ANSF? How many are remaining to be delivered in the contract?

Answer. There are 30 total Mi-17s under the current contract for the Afghan Special Mission Wing. Twenty-one Mi-17s have been delivered; nine remain to be delivered.

Question. What effect has the confrontation with Russia over Ukraine had on the willingness of Russian officials to work productively and cooperatively with their U.S. counterparts on issues relating to Syria?

◆ Has the level of Russian cooperation changed in recent weeks and if so, have these changes had any negative effects on U.S. interests?
◆ Do Russia's interests regarding Ukraine present opportunities for U.S. diplomacy vis-a-vis Syria?

Answer. Russia's actions in Ukraine do not appear to have had any effect on Russia's actions regarding Syria or its officials' willingness to work productively and cooperatively with the U.S. on issues relating to the Syria chemical removal effort. The level of Russian cooperation has not changed in recent weeks. The U.N./OPCW joint mission has removed 92 percent of Syria's declared chemical weapons and Russia has continued to encourage Syria to complete the removal of its chemical weapons from the remaining site.

It is in our own national interests to complete the removal of all chemical weapons from Syria, to work with the international community to respond to and prevent attacks on civilians, and to help bring an end to the bloodshed by assisting the Syrian people develop a political solution to the crisis. That said, Russian and U.S. views on broader Syria policy remain divergent. Russian support for the Assad regime has continued. Russia has been unable to convince the Assad regime to engage in direct negotiations that would lead to a Transitional Governing Body according to the Geneva Communique and the agenda set out for the Geneva II negotiations on a political solution to the Syrian conflict.

Question. Last year the U.S. took in 36 Syrian refugees, which is such a small number given the gravity and scale of this humanitarian crisis. The U.S. must accept significantly more, especially if we are to credibly ask other countries to accept more Syrian refugees as well.

◆ How will the State Department work with the Department of Homeland Security to significantly increase the number of Syrian refugees accepted by the United States?

Answer. UNHCR has begun to refer an increased number of Syrian refugee cases to the United States—the first step necessary to begin the resettlement process for any refugee. The pace of those referrals will increase in coming months and total thousands by the end of 2014. Refugees who are deemed eligible for admission to the United States will begin to arrive in 2015 and 2016. In line with U.S. policy, we expect we will accept a significant number of Syrian refugees over the next few years.

The Department of State directs, under established cooperative agreements, Resettlement Support Centers (RSCs) in Amman, Beirut, Istanbul, Baghdad, and Cairo that will process Syrian refugee referrals upon receipt from UNHCR. The U.S. Refugee Admissions Program is a deliberate process that involves many required steps, including an in-person Department of Homeland Security (DHS) U.S. Citizenship and Immigration Services (USCIS) interview, security checks, medical exams, and sponsorship assurance. DHS/USCIS adjudicating officers travel to most of these locations on a quarterly basis to adjudicate refugee cases in a timely fashion. The average processing time for a refugee resettlement case from referral to arrival in the United States is approximately 18–24 months.

It is important to note that any Syrian refugee who might be considered for admission to the United States will undergo the same intensive security screening that is applied to all refugees under consideration for U.S. resettlement. Refugee applicants are currently subject to more security checks than any other category of traveler to the United States, with security screening conducted by DHS and multiple U.S. Government intelligence, law enforcement, and defense agencies.

The Department of State works closely with DHS and the U.S. Government's law enforcement and intelligence vetting partners to ensure that only applicants who pass the rigorous security screening are admitted into the United States, that cases on security hold receive a timely review, and that those applicants who do not pass the security screening check are informed of their ineligibility to resettle in the United States.

Question. How does the administration hope to use the authority granted by Public Law 113–76 to support the Syrian opposition and pursue other Syria-related priorities? What amount of FY 2014 and prior year funding is currently available in the ESF account to support these efforts pursuant to the new authority? What tradeoffs and constraints does the administration face when considering the use of these funds? How does the administration plan to engage Congress regarding these funds?

Answer. The United States is providing nearly $287 million in nonlethal assistance to the Syrian opposition, drawing on existing accounts and authorities. The administration appreciates Congress' inclusion of expanded authority in the FY 2014 Appropriations Act (Public Law 113–76) which increases our ability to support the range of nonlethal support to civilian opposition groups. For example, we relied on this authority for our recent allocation of $26 million in FY 2013 ESF, notified to Congress on March 8. This funding will assist the Syrian opposition by expanding ongoing programs that support the SOC and its Assistance Coordination Unit's (ACU) priority campaigns inside Syria, including activities like the Syria In Green initiative, and those that provide critical search and rescue kits, civil defense materials, and communications equipment to support civil defense efforts in hard hit areas such as Aleppo City. (The Syria in Green initiative delivers urgently needed equipment and supplies like food baskets, generators, trucks, and school supplies.) Our programs will also provide financial and technical assistance to strengthen Syrian independent media, including 13 radio and television outlets.

The Department of State and USAID are currently assessing global funding availability through our FY 2014 allocation process, which seeks to balance our limited resources against our ongoing global commitments and priorities to determine how we will support key policy goals, such as those related to the Syria crisis. We will continue to engage and consult with Congress as these decisions are made.

Question. When does the administration expect to expend the remainder of the funds notified to the committee to date for assistance in Syria? For what purposes? In general terms, how will the $155 million in funds requested for FY 2015 assistance in Syria be used? How, if at all, will FY 2015-funded programs be different from programs implemented to date?

Answer. To date we have notified approximately $287 million in funding to support the Syrian opposition, of which approximately 65 percent has been delivered or is in-train. The spend rate for the remaining assistance depends on a variety of factors including access at the borders and other security considerations that are beyond our control. I therefore cannot speculate at exactly what point the remaining funds will be expended.

The administration's FY 2015 request for $155 million in funding to support the U.S. response to the Syria crisis will be used to continue ongoing opposition support efforts, including support to national- and local-level opposition groups as they strive to achieve and implement a negotiated political solution. Should a transition occur, U.S. assistance will help consolidate the political transition, support democratic processes, strengthen criminal justice institutions within Syria, and enable reconstruction and recovery efforts, in coordination with the other international donors. Some of these funds may also be used to help mitigate the economic, security, and infrastructure impacts of the ongoing crisis as well as the demands created by refugee flows into neighboring countries.

Question. What specific changes have been made to the oversight and implementation of U.S. assistance programs in Syria in light of the seizure of facilities held by U.S.-backed opposition groups in December 2013? What ''mission-specific'' activities will be carried out at U.S. facilities in Gaziantep and Adana, Turkey in line with the administration's request for $46.9 million in D&CP–OCO funding?

Answer. Since the December 2013 seizure of the Atmeh warehouse, we have been providing our nonlethal assistance for the moderate armed opposition directly to vetted unit commanders in the field rather than first warehousing equipment for later distribution. For our nonlethal assistance to civilian actors, our grantees and the final recipients of assistance, such as local and provincial councils and the ACU, we are constantly reevaluating routes and crossings to determine the safest options. After assistance is brought into Syria, opposition authorities often hire trucks to retrieve it, allowing councils to assess the checkpoints and actors along their routes and determine whether the roads are secure enough to return with the assistance. In one recent case, a relief committee from Ghouta on the outskirts of Damascus was scheduled to send trucks to pick up supplies but notified the ACU that they had to turn back after news of clashes en route to Homs. The trucks returned 2 days later and successfully collected the supplies. Councils and the ACU have also negotiated agreements with armed groups in the past to allow assistance to pass without interruption.

The Syria Transition Assistance Response Team (START), an interagency response team comprised of six offices and bureaus from State and USAID and which operates out of Mission Turkey, is responsible for coordinating and synchronizing U.S. assistance efforts given the fluid situation in Syria. It coordinates the planning and delivery of all nonlethal transition and humanitarian assistance and works with international organizations, NGOs, the Government of Turkey, and the Syrian opposition to ensure U.S. assistance effectively addresses Syria's needs. The FY 2015 D&CP–OCO funding request supports the personnel and operational cost components of the START.

Question. How are Function 150-funded programs coordinated with the Syria-related activities of other government agencies? How does the State Department view the prospect of using title 10 authorities and funds to support an overt train-and-equip mission for Syrian opposition-affiliated security personnel?

Answer. The Department of State and USAID regularly coordinate with our interagency colleagues in Washington, on both assistance and diplomatic efforts. Likewise, in the field, there is extremely close coordination among the various interagency elements providing assistance.

The President has repeatedly stated that no options have been taken off the table in our pursuit of a political settlement and a durable end to the violence in Syria, and I will work to preserve his flexibility and policymaking prerogatives as we evaluate the numerous options under discussion.

The administration acknowledges that the only durable solution to the crisis is a political transition. Until that happens, we are working with our partners to ensure that Syria's moderate opposition gets the help it needs to protect civilian populations from regime assault, enable civilian governance and service delivery, and contradict the influence of extremists. For the Department of State's part, we are providing approximately $80 million in nonlethal assistance to vetted, moderate armed groups in coordination with the Supreme Military Council (SMC). To date this aid has included cargo and pickup trucks, ambulances, food, communications gear, generators, tents, blankets, mattresses, medical kits and equipment, and specialized equipment such as forklifts and backhoes to units in both the north and south of Syria.

Question. Last week, Special Envoy Daniel Rubenstein announced that the U.S. Government notified the Syrian Government to suspend all operations at its Embassy and consulates in the United States, and that all diplomatic personnel must leave our country. However, Special Envoy Rubenstein's statement went on to say that, ''despite the differences between our governments,'' this announcement did not constitute a formal break in diplomatic relations because of ''our long-standing ties to the Syrian people.'' This announcement appears to recognize the Assad regime as the Syrian Government, however, in December 2012 Deputy Secretary Bill Burns recognized the Syrian Opposition Council as the legitimate representative of the Syrian people during the Friends of the Syrian People gathering in Morocco.

◆ Can you clarify the seeming contradiction between Special Envoy Rubensteins' statement and that of Deputy Secretary Burns?
◆ What effect will this action have on the millions of Syrians suffering inside and outside Syria?
◆ What actions is the administration taking to ensure that the SOC is viewed inside and outside Syria as the legitimate representative of the Syrian people?

Answer. The Friends of the Syrian People's recognition of the SOC as the sole legitimate representative of the Syrian people in December 2012 was a political step to underscore that we fully support it—not tantamount to recognition of the SOC as the new Government of Syria.

The Embassy had not been performing consular work for a long time when we decided to suspend its operations; we do not anticipate that it will have an operational impact on Syrians residing in the United States. We intend for the suspension to reinforce our public message that the Assad regime, which is waging war against its own people, is illegitimate.

Through senior-level meetings and other symbolic—but important—acts, we are trying to help strengthen the SOC. For example, we are expecting to receive a senior SOC delegation in Washington, DC, in the coming months, during which we hope to have productive discussions that further deepen our cooperation and understanding.

In addition to our ongoing diplomatic initiatives, the United States also seeks to help the SOC through our foreign assistance programs, which encourage it to strengthen ties with communities inside Syria. In this vein, we have successfully facilitated multiple SOC meetings with local councils, media outlets, and grassroots organizations over the past year.

We continue to provide assistance to local councils across Syria, an initiative that is implemented in close coordination with SOC's Assistance Coordination Unit (ACU). Our assistance helps the ACU strengthen its ability to respond to the needs of Syrians and conduct outreach inside Syria. With our help, the ACU has taken a lead role in determining the distribution of urgent equipment such as fire trucks, water bladders, ambulances, food baskets, and school supplies. The United States also provides operational support and resources to increase the SOC's connectivity to constituents, civil society, and local authorities, including funding to support their participation in the Geneva II process as well as outreach events such as townhall meetings, travel into Syria, and the establishment of satellite offices across Syria.

Question. To what extent do the constituent members of the Syrian Opposition Coalition hold varying views on questions of inclusiveness, protection of minorities, women's participation, disarmament, and relations with the United States and Israel? How have armed Islamist groups reacted to the coalition's participation in the Geneva discussions? What effect has the recent leadership changes and disputes in the Supreme Military Council had on the effectiveness of SMC-affiliated forces on the ground?

Answer. The SOC has made clear its views on the importance of political inclusiveness, protection of minorities, and women's participation. I would encourage you to review its proposal for a Transitional Governing Body, which it tabled at the second round of Geneva negotiations this past February, for insight into its commitment to these tenets. The SOC also presented a political platform of core principles which includes these elements.

We expect that a successor government will encourage widespread disarmament when the time comes for rebuilding. Many armed opposition figures have told us that they have no military background; their reason for fighting is self-defense, and they look forward to a period that will allow them to return to their prerevolution lives.

The SOC looks to the U.S. as a partner. We believe the SOC's legacy as represented in a successor government will work to curb violent extremism, bring stability and peace to the region, and normalize relations with neighbors.

There has been a mixed reaction across society regarding the proposition of Geneva Two negotiations. The Islamic Front, a conglomeration of the largest and most influential Islamist groups on the ground, met immediately before the Geneva talks began last January and decided not to criticize the process despite its reservations about the regime's intentions to negotiate. The SOC saw a surge of public support and was largely seen by its constituents and international partners alike as having effectively spoken for the Syrian people.

We do not believe that the SMC's leadership changes are likely to have a very significant impact on the ground. We have not seen any significant impact so far.

Question. What specifically is the U.S. doing now to use its influence with governments bordering Syria to ensure cross-border operations are better coordinated and implemented, so that these vital operations can be expanded to assist millions of people now not receiving aid?

Answer. As the Secretary noted during the May 15 London 11 meeting, the key obstacle to cross-border humanitarian assistance provision remains the Syrian Arab Republic Government (SARG). The SARG continues to prevent humanitarian aid deliveries, besiege villages, and bomb its own people in complete disregard of the unanimous demands in U.N. Security Council Resolution (UNSCR) 2139 and the demands of the international community. Despite these overwhelming obstacles, the U.N. and other humanitarian organizations are reaching millions in Syria each month, saving lives and providing medical care, food, clean water, and shelter in all 14 governorates. The United States commends the valiant efforts of these organizations and is committed to supporting their work.

The United States provides aid through all available channels—including U.N., international (IO), nongovernmental (NGO) and local humanitarian organizations—to those in need in Syria, no matter where they reside. As the single largest donor to the Syria humanitarian crisis, the United States is providing more than $1.7 billion in humanitarian assistance for those affected by the Syria crisis. Of this amount, we are providing nearly $340 million to support the work of NGOs inside Syria. The United States continues to work closely with humanitarian partners and other donors to determine the best ways to scale up humanitarian assistance in Syria, and continues to call on the SARG to fulfill its obligations under UNSCR 2139 and allow U.N. convoys to provide cross-border and cross-line aid.

Engaging the Governments of Turkey and Jordan

The U.S. Government works closely with the Government of Turkey (GOT) and the Government of Jordan (GOJ) in a joint effort to get aid to the 9.3 million people who need it in Syria. Our shared humanitarian goals include full implementation of UNSCR 2139 and increasing the amount of aid being brought into Syria. GOJ and GOT support has been essential in facilitating aid deliveries into Syria. We have also asked the Government of Turkey to expand registration for international NGOs that are involved in, or considering, cross-border assistance efforts (from Turkey into Syria).

Scaling Up Assistance to Syria

The Department and USAID continue to look for ways to get aid to as many people as possible inside Syria, particularly the 3.5 million people in hard-to-reach or besieged areas. To expand our reach, we want to increase the number of aid agencies with whom we work and expand our programs. We also continue to engage in robust discussions with IOs, NGOs, and other donors on how to deliver more assistance to those in need.

Question. The UNSC Resolution (S/RES/2139) and international humanitarian law provide the firm legal framework for implementing cross border operations. Last week, a U.N. convoy was able to restock aid supplies using the Nusaybin crossing into Northern Syria.

◆ (a) What do you see as the impact of U.N. Security Council Resolution 2139 (2014) to increase humanitarian access and aid delivery in Syria?

Answer. The unanimous adoption of U.N. Security Council Resolution (UNSCR) 2139 sent a strong signal to the Syrian Government that the Council wants to see action to address this catastrophic humanitarian crisis. The resolution has provided a stronger political basis for encouraging the U.N. to push harder for cross-border and cross-line assistance and established a process of monthly reports by the U.N.'s leading humanitarian coordination official to the Security Council.

The resolution calls for specific and concrete action from all parties to improve the humanitarian situation in Syria. Specifically, it calls for all parties to immediately lift the sieges on named populated areas, and demands that all parties, in particular the Syrian Government, promptly allow rapid, safe, and unhindered humanitarian access, including across borders, as well as immediately cease the indiscriminate use of horrific weapons, like barrel bombs, in populated areas.

At the same time, due to Russian opposition, the resolution was not adopted pursuant to the Council's authority under Chapter VII of the U.N. Charter and does not impose consequences for the government if it continues to block access. Russia continues to insist on using language in the Council that is strongly rooted in respect for state sovereignty and may be invoked to limit cross-border assistance in particular.

Humanitarian access inside Syria continues to be challenging The U.N. has repeatedly pressed for more cross-border access, particularly from specific crossing points in Jordan and Turkey, to deliver life-saving aid to populations that cannot be reached easily from Damascus. Most of these requests have been denied or gone unanswered by the government, depriving millions of people of desperately needed food, medical care, and supplies. In addition to the government, other armed groups—especially extremists—also bear responsibility for blocking aid delivery into some parts of Syria, and they, too, must be held accountable for their actions.

◆ (b) Please identify possible next steps by the Security Council.

Answer. The U.N. Security Council made clear its intent to consider further steps in the case of noncompliance with UNSCR 2139. U.N. Secretary General Ban Ki-moon has stated that failure to comply with the resolution's demands constitutes arbitrary denial of access and that the Security Council must take action. More than 2 months have gone by since the adoption of UNSCR 2139, with minimal progress in reaching millions of innocent civilians. The United States is actively involved in Council discussions regarding possible additional action to advance humanitarian access inside Syria, including a possible follow-on resolution.

◆ (c) What prevents the United Nations from sending more convoys into Syria?

Answer. The U.N. is limited in its ability to send additional convoys into Syria from neighboring states absent authorization from the government. The U.N.'s provision of international humanitarian assistance is guided by U.N. General Assembly Resolution 46/182 which states, among other things, that "the sovereignty, territorial integrity and national unity of States must be fully respected in accordance with the Charter of the United Nations. In this context, humanitarian assistance should be provided with the consent of the affected country and in principle on the basis of an appeal by the affected country." This resolution was adopted by consensus with support of the United States.

In addition, parts of Syria are controlled by terrorist and extremist groups who target international humanitarian aid workers and others seeking to provide assistance. General insecurity and the lack of guarantees by armed groups to safely enter areas make it very difficult for the U.N. to send convoys into the country.

◆ (d) Why does the U.N. continue to refuse to scale up its cross-border humanitarian operations given the massive scale of the civilian need, while smaller nongovernmental aid agencies routinely—and bravely—make cross-border deliveries to populations in desperate need?

Answer. Despite these real challenges, the U.N. continues to push the government to permit additional cross-border and cross-line access to people in need of aid and has sought to advance its work in every way possible. Some nongovernmental organizations (NGOs) are able to more easily provide cross-border assistance to some parts of the country because they are not required to strictly follow the U.N.'s procedures for delivery of humanitarian assistance, although they also face significant challenges. The U.S. is the largest humanitarian donor to Syria, providing $493.5 million to the U.N. and $384.5 million to NGOs, International Organizations and others working inside of Syria. We continue to push for greater coordination of the overall humanitarian effort to get us as much aid to the Syrian people as possible.

Question. What diplomatic efforts is the administration engaged in with regional states that have a role with respect to the current situation inside Syria to encourage the parties of the conflict to agree to allowing more humanitarian aid into Syria?

Answer. The administration is engaged in a broad range of diplomatic efforts with states that have influence over parties to the conflict inside Syria to work toward changing the situation on the ground and improving humanitarian assistance provision inside Syria. These diplomatic engagements include the United States robust participation in the High Level Group (HLG) on Syria Humanitarian Challenges. The Department also maintains continuous engagement at the highest levels with nongovernmental organization (NGO) and international organization (IO) partners involved in direct assistance provision.

The High Level Group (HLG) on Syria Humanitarian Challenges, initiated by U.N. Emergency Relief Coordinator Valerie Amos, was created shortly after the adoption of the October 2, 2013, U.N. Security Council Presidential Statement (PRST) on humanitarian access in Syria. The HLG, which currently has 31 member states, aims to mobilize member states with influence over the parties to the conflict to expand access for humanitarian actors to deliver aid to those in need in Syria, particularly the 3.5 million people trapped in besieged and hard-to-reach areas. The HLG has held seven plenary sessions, and the HLG subgroups have met regularly at the technical level in Geneva on a weekly or biweekly basis.

The subgroups have focused on seven priority areas including: increasing access to besieged areas; increasing access to hard-to-reach areas; expanding medical assistance and vaccination campaigns; demilitarizing schools, hospitals, and other civilian sites; streamlining administrative hurdles; increasing funding for U.N. humanitarian appeals; and working toward a political solution to the conflict through the Geneva II negotiations. While the group's efforts have not resulted in major access breakthroughs, it now serves the function of documenting noncompliance with UNSCR 2139, passed in February 2014, and keeping the international community focused on a specific set of tangible priority actions. The HLG is equally useful in publicly documenting the Syrian Government's responses (or lack thereof) to specific requests made by the U.N. for access to areas in need. The HLG thereby is building a body of evidence which, by determining that the SARG has "arbitrarily denied humanitarian aid" and committed violations of international humanitarian law, could pave the way for further steps in the Security Council that could ultimately break the impasse on access.

Most recently, at the May 15 London 11 Ministerial, Secretary Kerry joined fellow London 11 members to condemn the Assad regime for preventing the delivery of humanitarian assistance in Syria, particularly cross-border and cross-line access, and called for additional efforts by the international community to scale up humanitarian aid delivery into Syria, irrespective of the regime's consent.

Question. How many rounds of 30-day reporting does the administration expect the Secretary General to provide the Security Council to determine that humanitarian access is/is not improving? What sort of "further steps in the case of noncompliance" (per the language at the end of the UNSCR) will be discussed should the situation continue to remain the same (or deteriorate)?

Answer. The Secretary General has reported twice to the Security Council since the adoption of U.N. Security Council Resolution (UNSCR) 2139. During each session the United States has highlighted the Syrian Government's failure to fully and expeditiously implement the resolution. As the Secretary General stated in his recent report, 3.5 million people remain without access to essential goods and services. This is unacceptable. We are actively engaged in negotiations at the highest level to discuss possible next steps in case that the Syrian authorities continue to act inconsistently with UNSCR 2139. We want to ensure that further Security Council action would have a positive, tangible impact on humanitarian operations on the ground.

In addition to efforts in the Security Council, where Russian obstructionism may prevent further action, we are also engaged in other diplomatic efforts to improve people's access to humanitarian aid inside Syria. These diplomatic engagements include the United States active participation in the High Level Group (HLG) on Syria Humanitarian Challenges. The HLG was created by U.N. Emergency Relief Coordinator Valerie Amos shortly after the adoption of the U.N. Security Council Presidential Statement (PRST) on humanitarian access in Syria, issued October 2, 2013. The HLG aims to mobilize member states with influence over the parties to the conflict to expand access for humanitarian actors to deliver aid to those in need in Syria, particularly the 3.5 million people trapped in besieged and hard-to-reach areas. The HLG has held seven plenary sessions, and the HLG subgroups have met regularly at the technical level in Geneva on a weekly or biweekly basis.

While the group's efforts have not resulted in major access breakthroughs, the group serves a useful purpose in documenting nonimplementation of UNSCR 2139 and in keeping the international community focused on a specific set of tangible priority actions. The HLG is equally a useful exercise to publicly document the Syrian Government's responses (or lack thereof) to specific requests made by the U.N. for access to areas in need in order to build a body of evidence needed to determine the Syrian Government has violated international humanitarian law. Such a determination could pave the way for further steps in the Security Council or other fora.

RESPONSES OF AMBASSADOR ANNE PATTERSON TO QUESTIONS
SUBMITTED BY SENATOR BENJAMIN L. CARDIN

Question. The most recent U.N. Commission of Inquiry on Syria report indicates that grave breaches of international humanitarian law and significant violations of human rights law occur at an alarming frequency in Syria. Indiscriminate shelling, torture, massacres, blatant disregard for civilian immunity in warfare and other brutal acts are frequently reported. Many analysts have suggested that such patterns will continue until a political settlement is reached. Yet, with little progress having been achieved at the recent Geneva II talks, a political deal seems increasingly elusive.

◆ In your view, what can be done now to ensure accountability for crimes against humanity and war crimes committed during the Syrian conflict?

Answer. The United States has and will continue to call for accountability in Syria. For more than 3 years, we have consistently demanded a Syrian-led transitional justice and accountability process for atrocities in Syria, and supported institutions that are helping to build the foundation for future accountability efforts. We have encouraged other nations to highlight accountability in Syria and to support efforts to document abuses.

We have supported and engaged the independent international Commission of Inquiry on Syria (COI), which was established in 2011 by the U.N. Human Rights Council with a mandate to investigate violations of international human rights and war crimes in Syria. The COI is working to establish the facts and circumstances of such violations, which may include war crimes and crimes against humanity, and, where possible, to identify the perpetrators with a view to ensuring that they are held accountable.

We have also been instrumental in standing up the of the Syria Justice and Accountability Center (SJAC), which was established with the support of 40 countries to coordinate documentation on ongoing human rights abuses on all sides of the conflict. The SJAC is an independent, Syrian-led organization that collects, preserves, and analyzes information on alleged human rights violations and other relevant data to inform and contribute broadly to future transitional justice processes for Syria. Through a subgrant to the Syrian Commission for Justice and Accountability (SCJA), hundreds of thousands of documents and photos have been assembled to form the basis for a secure database for future use.

The United States maintains extensive sanctions on the Syrian regime, including sanctions targeting those responsible for human rights abuses.

Question. What mechanisms do you have in place to help appropriate Syrian stakeholders and other relevant parties identify and report on gross violations of human rights and war crimes in Syria?

Answer. The United States gives financial and material support to the Syria Justice and Accountability Center (SJAC). The SJAC was established with the support of 40 countries to coordinate documentation on ongoing human rights abuses on all sides of the conflict. The SJAC is an independent, Syrian-led organization that collects, preserves, and analyzes information on alleged human rights violations and other relevant data to inform and contribute broadly to future transitional justice processes for Syria. The SJAC is working with a network of Syrian human rights activists largely within Syria working on human rights documentation.

The SJAC's efforts are designed to contribute to all possible transitional justice mechanisms including truth-seeking, reparations, prosecution, reconciliation efforts, and memorialization, with the recognition that all of these efforts will be important in supporting the country's eventual recovery from this conflict.

The SJAC has also made a subgrant to the Syrian Commission for Justice and Accountability (SCJA). SCJA is currently reviewing hundreds of thousands of videos and Syrian regime documents for content related to chain of command and other factors that will assist accountability efforts. This information is being deposited into a secure database for future use.

In addition, the United States also supports organizations like Physicians for Human rights, which is training Syrian medical professionals to document sexual and gender-based violence and torture.

Question. What efforts has the United States taken to ensure accountability, including documenting, investigating and developing findings for war crimes committed during the atrocity for future prosecution?

Answer. The United States helped to establish the Syria Justice and Accountability Center (SJAC). The SJAC was established with the support of 40 countries to coordinate documentation on ongoing human rights abuses on all sides of the conflict. The SJAC is an independent, Syrian-led organization that collects, preserves, and analyzes information on alleged human rights violations and other relevant data to inform and contribute broadly to future transitional justice processes for Syria. The SJAC is working with a network of Syrian human rights activists largely within Syria working on human rights documentation.

The SJAC has also made a subgrant to the Syrian Commission for Justice and Accountability (SCJA). SCJA is currently reviewing hundreds of thousands of videos and Syrian regime documents for content related to chain of command and other factors that will assist accountability efforts. This information is being deposited into a secure database for future use.

The United States has supported the establishment and mandate renewal of the independent international Commission of Inquiry (COI) on Syria, which was established in 2011 by the U.N. Human Rights Council with a mandate to investigate violations of international human rights and war crimes in Syria. The COI is working to establish the facts and circumstances of such violations, which may include war crimes, atrocities, and crimes against humanity, and, where possible, to identify the perpetrators with a view to ensuring that they are held accountable.

RESPONSES OF ASSISTANT SECRETARY THOMAS COUNTRYMAN TO QUESTIONS
SUBMITTED BY SENATOR BENJAMIN L. CARDIN

On February 27, 2014, the United States Department of State issued its 2013 Human Rights Report on Syria, which described President Bashar al-Assad's use of ''indiscriminate and deadly force'' in the conflict , including the August 21, 2013, use of ''sarin gas and artillery to target East Ghouta and Moadamiya al-Sham, suburbs of Damascus, and killed over 1,000 people.''

Question. What other types of weapons, conventional and unconventional, have been used to perpetrate war crimes and crimes against humanity in Syria?

Answer. We continue to be gravely concerned by the Assad regime's indiscriminate attacks against the Syrian people. The Assad regime has engaged in unlawful attacks using a variety of means, including aerial bombing, artillery strikes, small arms fire, and, of course, chemical weapons.

Question. Are you tracking the origins of specific weapons? If so, what can you tell us about the origins?

Answer. We are following the support countries are providing to Syria, including weapons. The Russian Government continues to supply the Syrian regime, noting it is fulfilling its contracts with the government. Iran also continues to be a source of weapons. Separately, several countries in the region are providing assistance to the opposition. In addition, weapons have been smuggled out of Libya to Syria.

If you would like additional, more detailed information, we would be pleased to arrange a classified briefing.

ADDITIONAL MATERIAL SUBMITTED FOR THE RECORD

Letter Submitted by Syrian Opposition Coalition President Ahmad Jarba

الائتـــلاف الـوطنـــي لقــوى
الثورة و المعارضة السورية
National Coalition of Syrian
Revolution and Opposition Forces

Office of the President

March 25, 2014

The Honorable Robert Menendez (D-NJ)	The Honorable Robert Corker (R-TN)
Committee on Foreign Relations	Committee on Foreign Relations
United States Senate	United States Senate
Washington, D.C. 20510	Washington, D.C. 20510

Dear Mr. Chairman Menendez and Ranking Member Corker:

The situation in Syria is dire, and the people of Syria need the full support of the United States now more than ever. We acknowledge your efforts to bring attention to this issue in your recent letter to President Obama and by holding Committee hearings. For us, this issue is first and foremost about the dignity and democratic aspirations of the Syrian people, but we know it is also a critical issue for the security of the United States and its citizens and allies around the world.

Our Coalition is the broad alliance of Syrians united and dedicated to paving the way for a political transition from the dictatorship of Bashar al-Assad to a democracy that reflects the ethnic and religious diversity that is fundamental to Syria's heritage and its future. The Syrian people are looking to us and to the political process to bring an end to the killing and to stop Assad from demolishing and dismantling our country. The damage already done is overwhelming.

The Assad regime, backed by foreign fighters from the terrorist group Hezbollah and extremists imported from Iran, Iraq and elsewhere, has presided over the death of more than 140,000 Syrians. Almost half of the Syrian population—more than nine million civilians—have been forced from their homes. Dozens of cities and towns have been entirely demolished by regime air strikes and artillery bombardment.

The saddest part of this calculated catastrophe being carried out by Assad is what is happening to the children. There are over one million children refugees and thousands dead. According to UNICEF, more than five million children are at risk. For many of them, there is no school, there is no refuge; families have been decimated. Many children have been made orphans by Assad's war on the Syrian people. And what does the future hold for them?

We represent the best hope for their future. During the recent negotiations in Geneva, our delegation presented a detailed Statement of Principles that lays out a measured, realistic plan for the political transition, beginning with the establishment of a Transitional Governing Body (TGB) with full executive powers, formed on the basis of mutual consent, as required by the Geneva Communiqué and UN Security Council Resolution 2118. I have attached the plan to this letter for your reference.

We have made it clear publicly and on the ground: we reject terrorism and extremism, and we will continue to strengthen our resolve in doing so. We are undertaking a significant restructuring of our Supreme Military Command to increase the professionalism and effectiveness of our forces, and to ensure that they are fighting for a free and democratic Syria, and not to impose any political or religious ideology on Syrians. We need the help of the Senate and the US in this process.

On the ground, moderate opposition forces are fighting two fronts. On one front, we are fighting the regime and the extremist foreign militias that it has allowed to invade Syria, including Hizbollah, Iranians, and sectarian Iraqi militias. Meanwhile, Assad's policies continue to facilitate the influx of al-Qaeda backed fanatics, and our forces have opened up a second front to fight these unwelcome extremists, at the same time.

Senators, we believe the United States must be serious about enforcing UN Security Council Resolutions. The Assad regime has already missed numerous deadlines for eliminating its chemical weapons program as required by Resolution 2118, and the regime has failed to comply with the requirement in Resolution 2118 ¶ 16-17 that it "engage seriously and constructively" in the Geneva Conference, the goal of which is the full implementation of the Geneva Communiqué, "beginning with the establishment of a transitional governing body exercising full executive powers, which could include members of the present Government and the opposition and other groups and shall be formed on the basis of mutual consent." And over the last month, we have seen consistent failure by the regime to comply with the requirements of Resolution 2139, as well, which I will take this opportunity to describe.

Our Coalition has submitted information to the UN regarding compliance with UN Security Council Resolution 2139, despite difficult conditions on the ground. We have reiterated our commitment to support and abide by international humanitarian law. We are committed and seeking to ensure safe access for humanitarian aid to reach civilians anywhere in Syria. We look to the US to support us in these efforts, and we need more help in achieving the organizational reforms necessary to do so.

Meanwhile, Assad and his forces continue to commit war crimes and crimes against humanity. Resolution 2139 ordered the regime to stop its treacherous and indiscriminate campaign of barrel bombing, which causes death and unspeakable suffering to civilians and their homes. The regime has not complied, again flaunting a unanimous Security Council resolution because it has no serious enforcement mechanism, and Russia will ensure that remains the case. Resolution 2139 also requires the regime to stop arbitrary detention and torture, end its sieges, and allow humanitarian access. Instead, the regime continues to block humanitarian aid to thousands of desperate Syrians who are unable to receive food and medicine as long as they are sealed in their blockaded towns.

Humanitarian organizations are being driven out by fear. The continued recognition of Assad as the legal representative of the Syrian state by the US and the UN results in even supposedly neutral international aid being used to coax local communities to surrender without any political concessions or reforms. The US and the international community can begin to address this problem by further downgrading the regime's legal recognition, elevating the opposition's diplomatic recognition, and – with or without consent of the regime and Russia – enforcing the provisions of UNSCR 2139, which include: humanitarian access to all civilians, direct cross-border aid to Syria, and the immediate halt of barrel bombs and starvation sieges.

Senators, we want a political solution. We went to Geneva in order to seek a political solution. But while we presented our plan in Geneva, Assad's response was to escalate militarily. To our horror, more Syrians were killed during the time we tried to reason with his negotiators in Geneva than during any other previous comparable period of time. Assad's military dropped so many barrel bombs during the negotiations that Syrians began referring to these devastating weapons as "Geneva barrels."

You understand the complexity of the Syrian catastrophe, how it affects the broader Middle East and the potential consequences to our neighbors. Indeed, the crisis cannot be isolated from outside influences, nor can it be contained and ignored within our borders. The millions of refugees flooding into camps in Turkey, Jordan, Lebanon, and Iraq are having an enormous effect on those countries, while Syrians living in the tents of these camps wonder if they will ever go home or will live there the rest of their lives. And moreover, the same extremists and terrorists who we are fighting today are also determined to turn their aggression to you as well. With your committed support, we can stop them now, inside Syria.

On behalf of the democratic aspirations of the Syrian people, we implore you to take steps to help us fulfill those aspirations for a political transition in Syria. We welcome your country's generous provision of humanitarian aid, but more serious steps are also required.

We understand your limitations and concerns, but as willing and ready partners, we urge you to take concrete steps to: send a clear message to the Assad regime that there is no military solution to the struggle in Syria; send a clear message to Assad's base of supporters, showing clearly that the US and its allies are serious and committed to the political transition and enabling Syrians to establish the TGB in Syria; send a clear message to the Assad regime and to its base of supporters that achieving military advances on the ground will not make the regime legitimate, and it has lost its legitimacy to govern completely; strengthen the Coalition's capabilities in its fight against terrorist organizations and groups, as well as achieve a more balanced military position on the ground, to a level that creates enough pressure on the regime to push it towards a political settlement in Geneva; enable tangible humanitarian outcomes on the ground; and weaken the military capability and increase the political isolation of the regime and its allies. We need to work together to coordinate a long-term strategic plan for supporting the moderate opposition in its fight against the regime and a joint counter-terrorism plan against extremists from now until an agreement on political transition and a TGB can be reached. We need to work together to develop further our strategic plan for the security and stability of the transition, as well as for future relations between Syria and the US.

Senators, peace talks are stalled and the Assad regime remains committed to a military victory. The regime proved in Geneva that it has no inclination to talk about political transition. It has no incentive to talk in the absence of a recommitment to shifting the balance of power on the ground. Compelling them to negotiate on transition will require re-energized international support for the moderate opposition. Our forces remain committed to a political solution and are actively fighting international terrorist forces, while the regime has clearly indicated it will not accept the basis for political negotiations nor halt its strategy of mass atrocities.

Thank you for your continued leadership and support.

Sincerely,

Ahmad Jarba
President

cc: Senator Barbara Boxer   Senator James E. Risch
        Senator Benjamin L. Cardin   Senator Marco Rubio
        Senator Jeanne Shaheen   Senator Ron Johnson
        Senator Christopher Coons   Senator Jeff Flake
        Senator Richard J. Durbin   Senator John McCain
        Senator Tom Udall   Senator John Barrasso
        Senator Chris Murphy   Senator Rand Paul
        Senator Tim Kaine
        Senator Edward J. Markey

STATEMENT OF BASIC PRINCIPLES SUBMITTED BY
THE SYRIAN OPPOSITION DELEGATION

Geneva Peace Conference 9 February 2014
Syrian Opposition Delegation

Statement of Basic Principles

Agreement for a Political Settlement from the Geneva Peace Conference

9ᵗʰ of February 2014

Statement of Basic Principles

Agreement for a political settlement from the Geneva 2 Peace Conference:

In accordance with UN Security Council Resolutions 2042 (2012), 2043 (2012), 2059 (2012), and 2118 (2013); in fulfilment of the Final Communiqué of the Action Group for Syria of 30 June 2012 (the Geneva Communiqué); the Syrian opposition delegation to the Geneva Conference affirms that the participation of the two parties at the conference will not alone move the peace process forward; furthermore, the process requires the full implementation of the legal obligations resulting from international decisions and Security Council resolutions, in addition to the full and earnest implementation of general obligations of international humanitarian law, which will provide for the alleviation of the suffering of all of Syria's civilians, without discrimination; the appalling humanitarian situation on the ground must be improved; the implementation of these obligations will serve to build the Syrian people's confidence in the political negotiation process, in which both parties must show good faith and the political will to pursue the negotiations seriously; the primary objective of the Geneva 2 peace conference is the full implementation of the Geneva Communiqué of 30 June 2012, beginning with the establishment, on the basis of mutual consent, of a Transitional Governing Body with full executive powers over all ministries, agencies, and institutions of the State, including agencies, instrumentalities, and branches of the intelligence services, the military, armed forces, security forces and instrumentalities, and the police (thereby complying with Articles 16 and 17 of Security Council Resolution 2110 (2013)), the negotiations for the establishment of an interim Transitional Governing Body with full executive powers, and for the achievement of a political solution, will be guided by the following principles:

1. A political solution will be agreed upon by the two Syrian parties participating in the Geneva 2 peace conference, which will be considered an interim constitutional declaration.

2. The Transitional Governing Body will preserve the sovereignty and independence of the Syrian state and the full unity and territorial integrity of Syria. The Transitional Governing Body will take whatever decisions and steps are necessary to ensure the withdrawal of all external military groups and foreign fighters from the entire territory of Syria.

3. The Transitional Governing Body will constitute the sole legal representative of the sovereign and independent Syrian state, and it will be the only authorized representative of the Syrian state in international forums, and in all matters related to foreign affairs, and it will be bound by all international treaties and agreements signed by the Syrian state.

4. The primary objective of the Transitional Governing Body is the creation of a neutral environment for a political transition that will satisfy the legitimate aspirations of the Syrian people, in accordance with Articles 16 and 17 of Security Council Resolution 2118 (2013) and its second annex.

5. The Transitional Governing Body will implement, steer, and preside over an agreement to bring an end to violence in all its forms, and whereby it will take immediate steps to end armed violence, with a view to protecting civilians and achieving national stability, in the presence of international observers under the auspices of the United Nations.

6. The Transitional Governing Body will be obliged to carry out the transitional process in a way that provides security for all, in an atmosphere of stability and peace, which will require:

    I. The establishment of complete peace and stability, which requires all parties to cooperate with the Transitional Governing Body in guaranteeing a permanent end to violence, and will also include the completion of withdrawal operations, and addressing the matter of disarming and disbanding armed groups, or the integration of their members into the armed forces or public and civil services.

    II. Taking proactive steps to guarantee the protection and inclusion of all the constituent groups of the Syrian people, including Arabs, Kurds, Turkmens, Assyrian Syriacs, and others, in the transition process, to rebuild confidence and mutual respect, and to encourage political and social consensus with respect to the unity and stability of the Syrian state, territory, and people, similar to, for example, the agreement between the Syrian National Coalition and the Kurdish National Council.

    III. The continuity of state institutions, the employment of properly qualified state employees, and public services and institutions must be preserved, and they must be brought up to perform under international professional standards and in compliance with international human rights and labor laws. This will be done by studying and reforming their organizational structure and mission. These institutions will include the military and armed forces, all agencies and branches of the intelligence services, and the security apparatus. As a general principle, all state and public sector employees will keep their jobs. They will be returned to their positions, and guaranteed training programs, including retraining to increase their capacity if necessary. The state will remain committed to the creation of jobs and will maintain sources of income for all those currently employed. All the institutions of state, including the military, armed forces, intelligence services, and security services must operate in accordance with the rule of law and international professional and human rights standards. They will work under senior leadership that inspires public confidence, completely under the authority of the Transitional Governing Body.

7. The Transitional Governing Body will undertake a comprehensive economic, social, political, judicial and military strategy to bring about an end to violence by armed groups aligned with either of the two parties, or any other political, ideological, religious, sectarian or criminal persuasions, and prevent these groups from committing further violence.

8. The Transitional Governing Body will have full authority to allow immediate and full humanitarian access throughout the territory of Syria to international humanitarian organizations. No party will hinder the provision and delivery of humanitarian or medical assistance. All parties must cooperate under the leadership of the Transitional Governing Body to enable the evacuation of the wounded, and the return of refugees and displaced persons to their homes in Syria, with support from all parties.

9. The Transitional Governing Body will have the full power and authority to obtain lists of the names of all political prisoners, prisoners of conscience, prisoners arrested for participating in peaceful protests, and other detainees, and to provide for their release. Similarly, the Transitional Governing Body will have the right to review all criminal legislation issued after 15 March 2011, and the right to grant general and individual amnesty in accordance with law. The parties to this agreement are obliged to treat all detainees in accordance with international standards of human rights, until such time as these prisons, jails and detention centers are placed under the jurisdiction of the Transitional Governing Body. Likewise, they are obliged to report the location of all places of detention, jails and prisons, and not to obstruct international observers from visiting these locations. Likewise, all parties are obliged to communicate the fate of the missing and the kidnapped, the names of those who have died in these prisons, and their locations of burial.

10. The Transitional Governing Body, in order to achieve justice and strengthen the transition to peace and stability, will establish mechanisms to hold accountable those responsible for violations of human rights and international humanitarian law. The Transitional Governing Body will direct and lead all efforts aimed at achieving transitional justice and resolving social conflict according to the principles of justice and national reconciliation, and lead efforts to establish civil peace, and remove the seeds of discord among political parties and between civil and military groups at local levels. These goals will be realised through strong international support.

11. The Transitional Governing Body will have the full authority to ensure the rights, integration, and participation of all Syrians, regardless of religion, ethnicity, national origin or sect, in the process of decision-making and the implementation of its decisions.

12. The Transitional Governing Body will have full authority to ensure that the settlement agreement will be fully compatible with international standards of human rights, international law, humanitarian law, and democratic principles, and will contribute to regional security.

13. The Transitional Governing Body will put in place the main foundations and principles for implementation of the settlement agreement, in accordance with the democratic aspirations of the Syrian people and the rule of law.

14. The Transitional Governing Body will respect and guarantee: freedom of expression; the right to form associations, civil society organisations, and political parties; freedom to gather and hold peaceful protests and demonstrations; freedom of political participation; freedom of the press; and access by all Syrians to the media.

15. The Transitional Governing Body will guarantee the full participation and complete equality of Syrian women, in all rights and responsibilities.

16. The Transitional Governing Body will guarantee the right of equal citizenship for all Syrians without discrimination on the basis of their gender, religion, sect, ethnic origin, political affiliation or social status.

17. The Transitional Governing Body will take the appropriate steps to enable the Syrian people to decide its own future. This will include the participation of all sectors and components of society in a national reconciliation conference, which independent, international civil society organisations will be invited to observe, in accordance with agreed mechanisms. This process will include all Syrians, be of the highest national import, and will produce a body of principles that will serve as the foundation of the new constitution that will be agreed by a future elected constituent assembly.

18. The Transitional Governing Body will make arrangements for the election of a constituent assembly in accordance with the electoral system decided in the settlement agreement, with observation by independent international civil society organizations.

19. The Transitional Governing Body will make arrangements for the conduct of a referendum on the constitution drafted by the constituent assembly, which will be supervised under the auspices of the United Nations, and the constitution will need to be ratified by a two-thirds majority of voters.

20. After the establishment of a new constitutional regime by the Syrian people through referendum, the Transitional Governing Body will undertake preparations for free and fair multi-party elections in accordance with the terms of the constitution, under the direct supervision of the constituent assembly and observation by international civil society organizations.

21. The Transitional Governing Body will dissolve immediately upon the assumption of constitutional powers by the elected executive bodies.

22. The constituent assembly will disband immediately upon the holding of the first parliamentary session of the elected parliament.

23. The Transitional Governing Body will work to coordinate with the UN Security Council and the international community on ensuring compliance with its decisions and to guarantee complete support for the Transitional Governing Body from Arab, regional, and international actors.

24. The Transitional Governing Body will apply such neutral and independent standards and metrics as are recognized by the UN Security Council, for the evaluation of the application of the agreement, as well as any subsequent agreements in accordance with Articles 16 and 17 of UN Security Council Resolution 2118 (2013). In case of non-implementation of the agreement, application of measures provided in Chapter 7 of the UN Charter will be necessary (as stipulated by Article 21 of UN Security Council Resolution 2118 (2013)).

———

STATEMENT SUBMITTED BY SAVE THE CHILDREN

Syria's three year civil war has had a devastating impact on children. At least 1.2 million children have fled the conflict and become refugees in neighboring countries, while another 4.3 million children in Syria are in need of humanitarian assistance. Children have witnessed and experienced extreme violence, and more than 10,000 young lives have been lost.

It is not just the bullets and the shells that are killing and maiming children. They are also dying from the lack of basic medical care. As documented in Save the Children's report entitled, ''A Devastating Toll,'' Syria's health system has been devastated by the war. As a result, increasing numbers of children are suffering and dying from diseases that would previously either have been treated or prevented from taking hold in the first place.

Across Syria, hospitals, clinics and pharmacies have been attacked and destroyed. Sixty percent of hospitals and 38 percent of clinics are no longer functioning. In Aleppo, a city that should have 2,500 doctors, only 36 remain. Production of life-saving medicines has fallen by 70 percent.

The few remaining facilities struggle to cope with the large number of patients who need treatment. Health workers, medical staff and patients, including children, have come under attack either en route to or inside medical facilities themselves. Homes are being used as makeshift hospitals, even turning living rooms into operating theaters.

The impact on children is horrific. Children are having limbs amputated because the clinics don't have the equipment to treat them. Newborn babies are dying in incubators due to power cuts. Doctors are reported to be knocking out patients with metal bars for lack of anesthetics.

Deadly diseases, such as measles and meningitis, are on the rise. Even polio, which was eradicated across Syria almost 20 years ago, is now being carried by up to 80,000 children across the country. Moreover, since the outbreak of the war, far too many children have died because they can't get treatment for life-threatening diseases such as cancer, epilepsy, diabetes and kidney failure.

Serious steps must be taken to relieve the suffering of children in this conflict. To this end, we urge policymakers to take the following actions:

1. Ensure that United Nations Security Council Resolution 2139 on humanitarian access is implemented immediately, to provide vaccines, food, water, medicines and other life-saving assistance. Humanitarian organization must have freedom of access in all areas. Aid must be allowed to cross conflict lines, enter besieged areas, through humanitarian pauses if necessary, and cross borders where this is the most direct route.

2. Use diplomatic pressure to urge all parties to the conflict to cease targeting health facilities and to cease attacks on medical personnel to ensure that children can access medical treatment.

3. Provide immediate investment in, and access to, child-focused health services to ensure that children are not dying from preventable and treatable injuries and illnesses.

The international community is failing Syria's children, even as they are injured and wounded and are unable to access treatment, as they contract polio and other preventable diseases that kill and disfigure them, and as they suffer and die from not being able to get the right medicine. World leaders must stand up for the smallest victims of this conflict and send a clear message that their suffering and deaths will no longer be tolerated.

————

STATEMENT SUBMITTED BY ANDREA KOPPEL, VICE PRESIDENT, GLOBAL ENGAGEMENT AND POLICY, MERCYCORPS

Mercy Corps is an Oregon-based humanitarian and development nonprofit organization working in over 40 countries. Our mission is to alleviate suffering, poverty and oppression by helping people build secure, productive and just communities. For over 30 years, Mercy Corps has had a presence in the Middle East, working together with local partners to address humanitarian and protection needs, build the capacity of local and national governments, mitigate violence, and address the specific needs of children and youth.

We greatly appreciate the attention this committee has paid to the Syrian crisis, and particularly, Chairman Menendez and Ranking Member Corker, for their leadership in highlighting the issues facing Syria, as well as its neighbors. As the crisis enters its fourth year, and as refugees continue to leave Syria en masse, the fabric of the Middle East is being dramatically altered. The number of Syrian refugees is estimated to reach 4 million by the end of 2014. One in four people living in Lebanon is already a Syrian refugee. And, Jordan's scarce natural and financial resources have been stretched to a breaking point.

From our experience working in Syria and the refugee hosting countries of Iraq, Jordan and Lebanon, we believe it is imperative that the U.S. assistance policies shift gears and develop an integrated strategy that moves beyond basic provision of humanitarian assistance. The gravity of the challenge, and the shortage of funds,[1] require that donor resources are spent smarter and more efficiently. To address the impact that this protracted crisis is having on the region, we urge you to support the following recommendations:

(1) Recalibrate the response strategy to strategically fund and integrate relief and development

To date, the bulk of the response efforts have focused on quick impact humanitarian response efforts, often at the detriment of development goals and the ability of refugee hosting communities to address and plan for the long-term consequences. Moving forward, the U.S. Government must align and equally prioritize development and humanitarian accounts and ensure they complement each other.

Mercy Corps' recently released paper, ''Tapped Out: Water scarcity and refugee pressures in Jordan,'' provides a good case study to illustrate the pressures that the crisis is placing on the resources—both natural and financial—of countries and communities throughout the region. Prior to the crisis Jordan's water supply was already on the edge of crisis and the country had been over-exploiting groundwater basins for a generation. Aquifer levels were declining at a rapid rate—over two meters a year in some places. Population growth, economic development, and climate change had placed dangerous burdens on precious supplies. Due to aging infrastructure, 76 billion liters of water a year—enough to meet the needs of 4 million people—are lost to leakage. Now, Jordan is running out of water. Refugee pressures have accelerated and complicated this trend and Jordan is drying up more quickly. As competition for scarce resources rises, tensions are also on the rise—both between refugees and hosts, as well as between host communities and their own governments. While recognizing the significant contributions the U.S., including the Millennium Challenge Corporation (MCC), has made to Jordan, we would recommend future U.S. investments scale-up in the following areas: (a) infrastructure improvements that focuses on needed repairs to key service sectors like water and health facilities; (b) repairs of existing infrastructure and training for maintenance personnel to preserve investments; (c) capacity building at the local, regional and national level for joint planning and community outreach; and (d) application of a conflict lens to all new initiatives. These types of interventions require long-term investments and funding. If done smartly, development support can mitigate the need for costly short-term fixes.

(2) Build the resilience of refugees and host communities

As part of the U.S. response, we must emphasize ''resilience'' that is, building the capacity of communities to learn, cope, adapt, and transform in the midst of this crisis. Increasing the ability of communities to adapt and respond to shocks and stresses requires more than simply digging a well or building a new school. A cornerstone of the U.S.'s policy in responding to the Syria crisis must be a focus on supporting local institutions and build cross-community partnerships between refugees and host-communities. The U.S. Congress should encourage USAID, State, and other donors to invest in programs that support local actors who can ultimately manage, design, and implement programs that work in tandem with national response plans, and programs that strengthen partnerships between government and civil society. This will ensure that U.S. interventions are not just Band-Aids, but have a sustainable impact in the region.

(3) Invest in adolescents

From our grassroots experience—and based on the findings of a recent Mercy Corps assessment on adolescents in Lebanon—we are seeing an entire generation of young people's dreams and opportunities for the future placed at risk. According to UNICEF, the crisis inside Syria affects 4.65 million children and an additional 1 million children have fled their country because of the violence, now living as refugees in camps and host communities in neighboring countries. Many of these refugees are in their adolescence, a time of life-changing biological and psychosocial events, and face uncertain futures because of the shocks and stresses of war, educational disadvantages, exposure to violence, and gender discrimination.

Mercy Corps is concerned the growing number of adolescent refugees are not supported adequately by assistance programs. We call on Congress to increase funding for programs targeting adolescent refugees to address their unique psychosocial and developmental needs, including through programs that promote tolerance, build conflict mitigation and management skills, and strengthen young people's community engagement through involvement in quick-impact community projects.

We appreciate the opportunity to present these recommendations, drawn from our on-the-ground experiences in the region, recent policy papers and assessment reports.[2] Thank you again for the much-needed attention this committee has paid to the crisis and for your efforts to improve the lives of the Syrian people and their neighbors.

Notes

¹ For details on the most recent consolidated appeal, see online at: http://www.data.unhcr.org/syria-rrp6/regional.php.

² Mercy Corps recent policy papers include: "Rethinking the Syrian Refugee Response" available online at: http://www.mercycorps.org/research-resources/charting-new-course-re-thinking-syrian-refugee-response and "Tapped Out: Water Scarcity and Refugee Pressures in Jordan" available online at: http://www.mercycorps.org/research-resources/tapped-out-water-scarcity-and-refugee-pressures-jordan. Mercy Corps' assessment on adolescents is forthcoming and will be published and available online in April, 2014.

STATEMENT SUBMITTED BY DR. CAROLYN Y. WOO, PRESIDENT AND CEO, CATHOLIC RELIEF SERVICES

"Too many lives have been shattered in recent times by the conflict in Syria, fueling hatred and vengeance. Let us continue to ask the Lord to spare the beloved Syrian people further suffering, and to enable the parties in conflict to put an end to all violence and guarantee access to humanitarian aid."
Pope Francis' Christmas day message *Urbi et Orbi.*

As President and CEO of Catholic Relief Services, I provide this written statement today to share the perspective of Catholic Relief Services (CRS), the official humanitarian agency of the Catholic community in the United States.

Chairman Menendez, Ranking Member Corker, thank you for holding the hearing "Syria after Geneva: Next Steps for U.S. Foreign Policy." With the Church across the globe, we solemnly mark the third anniversary of the beginning of this war and call for a renewed diplomatic effort to end the horrific bloodshed that has killed more than 130,000 people. While our staff and partners in the region are heroically responding to the human needs on the ground, their courage and commitment must be matched by an equal resolve to end this conflict.

CRS and our partners are privileged to serve more than 350,000 beneficiaries in response to the Syrian conflict, programming over $60 million in assistance. About one-quarter of those funds are from U.S. Government agencies, and another quarter from private U.S. individuals and foundations. This testimony is based on CRS' experience responding to human needs throughout the region.

As you consider next steps in U.S. foreign policy, CRS makes three main recommendations:

(1) Recommit to serious negotiations to find a political solution to the crisis, ensure impartial and neutral humanitarian assistance, and seek to rebuild an inclusive society in Syria that protects the rights of all its citizens, including Christians and other minorities.

(2) With donor governments and refugee host countries, develop and fund a coordinated, long-term humanitarian and development strategy for the region, including a contingency plan and a plan for the resettlement of refugees.

(3) Continue to prioritize adherence to international humanitarian law, especially to protect civilians, lift all sieges, and facilitate humanitarian access.

RECOMMIT TO A POLITICAL SOLUTION

The conflict in Syria is among the worst in more than a generation. More than 130,000 people have been killed. The use of chemical weapons, barrel bombs, systematic torture, and violence against women has cause extreme suffering among countless victims. Traumatized, as many as 2.6 million people have fled Syria. More than 9 million people are in need.

With Pope Francis, we believe pursuit of military solutions is futile and will distract from serious diplomatic and political solutions. I reiterate the policy of the U.S. Conference of Catholic Bishops: "The longstanding position of our Conference of Bishops is that the Syrian people urgently need a political solution that ends the fighting and creates a future for all Syrians, one that respects human rights and religious freedom." ¹

The Bishops continue to "ask the United States to work with other governments to obtain a cease-fire, initiate serious negotiations, provide impartial and neutral humanitarian assistance, and encourage building an inclusive society in Syria that protects the rights of all its citizens, including Christians and other minorities." ²

It is CRS' experience that Syrians are proudly moderate, educated, and cultured; a peaceful solution is possible. The solution, of course, lies within Syria, but the United States and the international community must do all we can to help.

As a critical component of a diplomatic framework on Syria, the donor community must work with donor governments and refugee host countries to develop and fund a coordinated, long-term humanitarian and development strategy for the region, including a contingency plan and a plan for refugee resettlement.

Outside of Syria, the region remains relatively stable given the enormous movements of people it is experiencing. The United Nations Office for the Coordination of Humanitarian Affairs (UNOCHA) put forth its largest humanitarian appeal ever in December, with $6.5 billion for the Syria response. Since the Kuwait Donor Pledging Conference in January, where $2.3 billion was pledged for Syria, only 14 percent of the appeal has been funded. The United States has been generous, but needs continue to grow. Through the FY 2015 appropriations process, Congress should provide robust humanitarian assistance to Syria at no less than FY 2014 levels.

By coordinating assistance with other donors, the international community can improve the efficacy of assistance. U.S. Government assistance to date has been critical, and it must continue to lead, given the immense need. The U.S. Government should particularly engage Gulf States and other donors who could help fund the scale-up of programming. Donors should scale-up program funding to help restore livelihoods of refugees who will likely not return home soon; educate children who have already lost so much; and restore psycho-social support and peacebuilding programming to respond to emotional needs. As the United States own history with conflict has taught us, often the least visible wounds take the longest to heal.

In addition to much needed humanitarian assistance, bilateral and development assistance will help neighboring countries to keep their borders open. While Jordan, Lebanon, Turkey, Egypt, and other countries have been extremely generous and hospitable to their Syrian neighbors fleeing the conflict, these societies are under extreme strain from the added burden of serving refugees, most of which are not in camps, but are living amidst the local population.

Even when the conflict ends, the humanitarian need will be serious for years. The United States must support local institutions in refugee hosting countries, such as the schools and hospitals, both public and private, which have expanded services to accommodate refugees from Syria. Each country situation is different, but the consistent theme is that schools and hospitals cannot handle both the local population and the continued influx of refugees. Integration of humanitarian and development funding can ensure that needs of both vulnerable host communities and refugees from Syria are met.

This long-term strategy should include a commitment to resettle refugees, especially vulnerable populations. Women and children are at risk for trafficking. As many as 4,000 unaccompanied refugee minors are in Jordan and Lebanon. Religious minorities, who have played a moderating role in the politics of the region, feel caught. And thousands of Iraqis who fled to Syria are now displaced a second time. These groups require particular attention which can be difficult to come by in communities accommodating so many refugees.

The U.S. Government should resettle its fair share of refugees as part of this strategy, including 15,000 this year alone. We urge the Department of Homeland Security, in consultation with the Department of State and the Department of Justice, to remove expeditiously unjust impediments to U.S. resettlement by implementing discretionary authority to grant exemptions from overly broad terrorism related inadmissibility grounds (TRIG) of U.S. immigration law. I recommend to you the testimony by Most Reverend Eusebio Elizondo, M. Sp. to the Subcommittee on the Constitution, Civil Rights and Human Rights on January 7, 2014, on behalf of the United States Conference of Catholic Bishops.

Diplomatic efforts must continue to exhort parties to the conflict to adhere to international humanitarian law, especially to lift sieges, protect civilians, and facilitate humanitarian access.

Humanitarian assistance should not require negotiation, but the dignity and very lives of people on the ground require that any party with the power to ensure humanitarian access does all it can. Since the passage of U.N. Security Council Resolution 2139 in late February, parties to the conflict continue to impede humanitarian assistance.

Hundreds of thousands of people remain under siege in cities across Syria. No diplomatic means should be spared to exhort parties to the conflict to lift sieges. Until sieges are lifted, it is critical to secure safe and unhindered evacuation of those who wish to leave. Convoys with food and critical medicines must be allowed unfettered access to those under siege. And vaccination campaigns must be permitted to continue.

Even in areas not under siege, humanitarian access remains byzantine. The Assad regime must make good on its commitment to streamline processes for humanitarian assistance. The U.S. Government and other donors must work closely with countries neighboring Syria to provide cross-border access to millions of people in hard to reach places. Days of truce and pauses in fighting to allow for humanitarian assistance would help immensely.

Dozens of humanitarian workers and medical care providers have been killed in Syria. To avoid more deaths, humanitarian assistance must remain impartial and neutral. Exemptions for humanitarian organizations to U.S. branding requirements are critical. Even the perception of affiliation of humanitarian assistance with the West can endanger humanitarian workers. The perception of biased aid emboldens the Assad regime to encumber aid.

Finally, all diplomatic means must be undertaken to recover the civilian nature of key institutions. Schools and hospitals have been militarized and therefore targeted. The lives of Syrians are at risk, as is the future of those fortunate enough to survive.

Mr. Chairman and Ranking Member, thank you for your attention to the concerns of Catholic Relief Services and our partner agencies. I join the United States Conference of Catholic Bishops in urging you to recommit to serious negotiations toward a political solution to the conflict in Syria. To help our international assistance reach more people, I recommend that you work with other donors to develop a longer term regional strategy. I ask you to work with the Committee on Appropriations subcommittees for State, Foreign Operations and Related Programs and Agriculture to adequately fund the humanitarian response in Syria. And I urge you to work with the Judiciary Committee so that the United States can do its part to resettle the neediest refugees. Please exhort parties to the conflict, and those who influence them, to adhere to international humanitarian law and protect civilians and humanitarian workers. The very stability of the entire region requires us to achieve these goals.

In closing, I echo the words of Pope Francis' Vigil for peace, ". . . I think of the children: look upon these . . . look at the sorrow of your brother, stay your hand and do not add to it, rebuild the harmony that has been shattered." When we look back at our response to the crisis in Syria, let us say we did all we could.

Notes

[1] Most Reverend Richard E. Pates, Bishop of Des Moines and Chair of the Committee on International Justice and Peace of the United States Conference of Catholic Bishops, letter to Secretary of State John Kerry, August 29, 2013.

[2] U.S. Conference of Catholic Bishops Administration Committee Statement on Syria, September 10, 2013.

STATEMENT SUBMITTED BY THE COALITION FOR A DEMOCRATIC SYRIA

RUSSIA WILL NOT PLAY A CONSTRUCTIVE DIPLOMATIC ROLE

On February 3, 2012, the Assad regime unleashed an unprecedented artillery bombardment on the Baba Amr area of Homs, then the power center of the Syrian opposition. Two days later, after the bloodiest 48 hours of the Syrian Revolution to date, Russia and China vetoed action on the United Nations Security Council to stop the slaughter.

In the aftermath of this infamous double-veto, President Barack Obama declared "Any government that brutalizes and massacres its people does not deserve to govern." However, the statement of then-U.N. Ambassador Susan Rice better encapsulates U.S. policy since February 2012. Referring to the decisions of Russia and China to veto, she stated, "Any further bloodshed that flows will be on their hands."

The primary component of U.S. policy toward Syria since 2012 has been to shame Russia into easing its client dictator out of power, by reminding Russian President Vladimir Putin that the blood of Syrians lies on his hands. Since Ambassador Rice's statement, the death toll in Syria has risen from 7,500 to nearly 150,000. The Assad regime's crackdown has escalated to include aerial bombardments, Scud missiles, and chemical weapons. Syrians have suffered a historic humanitarian crisis worse than that of the Rwanda Genocide, including the first major chemical weapons attack in 25 years.

Through all this, Russia has continued to back Assad to the hilt, even shipping offensive weapons to the regime on the eve of Geneva II talks this January. Yet Obama administration policy has relied, against all logic, on the hope that Putin could be shamed into abandoning his client in Damascus.

EVENTS IN CRIMEA HAVE ORIGINS IN SYRIA

It took the massacre of peaceful protesters in Kyiv by Putin's client Viktor Yanukovych, followed by the brazen Russian annexation of Crimea, for administration officials to finally grasp what Syrians have known for three years: Putin has no shame, and has no qualms supporting bloodshed on a massive scale.

Syrian Americans were not surprised when Putin shrugged off the U.S.'s stern diplomatic warnings against aggressive action in Ukraine. The U.S. had delivered similar diplomatic warnings to the Assad regime before, and the regime had safely ignored each one, crossing red line after red line. In fact, each major diplomatic initiative on Syria has ended with an unprecedented military escalation by the Assad regime:

- From November 2011–January 2012, Arab League observers entered Syria to help implement a cease-fire agreement between the regime and the Syrian opposition. The following month, Assad forces commenced unprecedented artillery assaults on Bab Amr.
- From April 2012–May 2012, rebel Free Syrian Army forces observed a ceasefire as part of the Geneva Plan negotiated by UN–Arab League envoy Kofi Annan. In late May, Assad's "Shabiha" paramilitaries killed over 100 civilians at Houla in the worst massacre to date.
- In May 2013, Secretary of State John Kerry attempted to revive diplomatic talks in what was then dubbed "Geneva II." That same month, Hezbollah forces openly invaded Syria for the first time to overtake the city of Qusair. Hezbollah has since deployed throughout the country, tipping the balance of the war and enflaming sectarian tensions across the region.
- On August 18, 2013, U.N. inspectors arrived in Damascus to investigate prior small-scale chemical weapons attacks. Three days later, the Assad regime killed over 1,500 civilians in its infamous Ghouta chemical attacks.
- During "Geneva II" transition talks from January 22–February 17, Assad forces escalated their attacks with unprecedented barrel bombings. The three weeks of Geneva II talks were the bloodiest period in the history of the Syrian Revolution.

By the time Ukrainian President Viktor Yanukovych fled Kyiv on February 22, his backer Vladimir Putin knew that Russia could annex Crimea without risk of a damaging response from the United States. If Iran and its Hezbollah proxies could safely invade Syrian territory at Qusair with no penalty, why would it be any different for Russia in Crimea?

THE UNITED STATES NEEDS A MORE ASSERTIVE POLICY

By centering its Syria policy on Assad and Putin, in the futile hope that one or both would respond to diplomacy, the U.S. has lost a great deal of global credibility. The consequences of this lost credibility can be expected to increase, as transnational extremists flood into Syria and Russian troops mass in western Crimea. Yet the U.S. can begin to restore its lost credibility by revamping its Syria policy, and taking the following steps:

1. Withdraw legal recognition from and sever diplomatic ties to the Assad dictatorship

Withdrawing diplomatic ties would send a firm statement to the international community that war crimes like Assad's have consequences, and would encourage defections from regime forces.

The Syrian American community encourages Congress members to support H. Res. 520, which urges the Administration and U.S. allies to "formally withdraw their recognition of Bashar al-Assad's regime as the rightful Government of Syria, unless and until the Assad regime and its supporting militias discontinue their barbaric slaughter." We also encourage the introduction of a companion bill in the Senate.

2. Demand that the Obama administration explain its plan to address the deteriorating situation

The lack of a clear U.S. policy on Syria in the face of escalating violations by Assad, Hezbollah, Iran and Russia gives these violators a dangerous sense of impunity with far-reaching implications. Syrian Americans wish to see the formulation of such a policy as soon as possible.

We urge Congress Members to support H. Res. 520 and S. Res. 384, each of which calls on the President to develop and submit to Congress within 90 days "a strategy for United States engagement on the Syria crisis, with a specific focus on humanitarian assistance and development, and protecting human rights in Syria and in the region."

3. Use H. Res. 520, S. Res. 384, and U.N. Security Council Resolution 2139 to pressure both Assad and Russia on the provision of humanitarian access to besieged areas

Both H. Res. 520 and S. Res. 384 urge ''unfettered access to humanitarian aid throughout the Syrian Arab Republic, respecting the safety, security, independence, and impartiality of humanitarian workers and ensuring freedom of movement to deliver aid.'' UNSC Resolution 2139 demands that ''all parties, in particular the Syrian authorities, allow rapid, safe, and unhindered U.N. humanitarian access for U.N. humanitarian agencies across conflict lines.''

UNSC 2139 is of particular note because even Russia endorsed it, yet Assad continues to deny humanitarian assistance. The United States can restore some of its lost international credibility by pressuring Russia to live up to its word. Congress can push the Administration to back enforcement of UNSC 2139 by passing H. Res. 520 and S. Res. 384.

———